GOD
IS NOT
A VENDING
MACHINE

... SO WHY
DO WE PRAY
LIKE HE IS?

GOD
IS NOT
A VENDING
MACHINE

...SO WHY
DO WE PRAY
LIKE HE IS?

Marvin D. Hinten

ZONDERVAN
PUBLISHING HOUSE
OF THE ZONDERVAN CORPORATION
GRAND RAPIDS, MICHIGAN 49506

Library of Congress Cataloging in Publication Data
Hinten, Marvin D.
    God is not a vending machine—so why do we pray like He is?

    Includes index.
    1. Prayer. I. Title.
BV210.2.H57 1983   248.3'2   83-10350
ISBN 0-310-47081-1

Printed in the United States of America

83 84 85 86 87 88 / 9 8 7 6 5 4 3 2 1

CONTENTS

PREFACE

THE LOAN HAD FALLEN THROUGH.

After weeks of excited planning, my wife Audrey and I had just discovered we would not be able to buy our first house after all. She was taking it calmly, reading *Winnie-the-Pooh and the Blustery Day* to three-year-old Rocky in the living room; I, a little less maturely, was sulking in the back bedroom of our trailer. Rocky, an energetic and talkative blonde, had apparently noticed my depression.

"Is Daddy sad, Mommy?" Rocky asked.

"Yes, he is," my wife replied.

"Can I go help him feel better?" Rocky queried.

"Daddy might want to be left alone," Audrey answered, "but you can go see."

Rocky toddled to the back bedroom and knocked on the door. "Daddy, Mommy said I could come in."

I recognized that as a slight exaggeration but let him in anyway. "Are you sad, Daddy?"

"Yes, I sure am," I admitted.

"Why?" he asked.

I explained to Rocky that we would not be able to buy a house because we couldn't get enough money, and this made me feel very sad.

"Can I pray for you to feel better, Daddy?" he asked.

Anxious to encourage his relationship with God, I nodded. Rocky lay down on the bed, closed his eyes, and said two sentences.

"Dear Jesus, thank you that we don't have enough money to buy a house. And thank you that some day we'll have enough money to buy a house. Amen."

I am not sentimental. But on that day I wept hot tears in my bed and hugged the son who showed me the attitude God wanted. Of course, Rocky was only repeating what he'd heard. If a favorite toy broke, we would pray as a family in thankfulness for the happy times we had had with it. If Audrey were sick, we would all thank God that He was keeping her spirits up. Rocky had learned from us, over and over, that prayer is not chiefly a series of requests, but a grateful joy for God's graciousness under all circumstances.

"Thank you that we don't have enough money to buy a house." That's what this book is about. We miss most of prayer's benefits because we often see it chiefly as a time to present God with the day's shopping list.

This book is not only to be read; it is to be used in building up your private and interpersonal prayer life, making it—and yourself—more pleasing to God. When we really love someone, our chief desire is to please that person. Specific suggestions for doing this are found at the end of most chapters as "Putting Prayer Into Practice." These are only suggestions; the goal is not to learn a certain way of praying, but to know, appreciate, and glorify God.

I gratefully acknowledge the people in our prayer group who helped me explore the goodness of God: Alex and Ronda Miller, Gordon and Marcia Schmidt, Adrian and Linda Adam, Mark and Debbie Bilansky, Jerry and Sally Smith, Sharon Brownback, Jerry and Donna Noble, and my wife Audrey, who cheerfully typed the manuscript as well.

GOD
IS NOT
A VENDING
MACHINE

...SO WHY
DO WE PRAY
LIKE HE IS?

God Is Not a Vending Machine

1

WHEN MY EVENING COMPOSITION CLASS HAS ITS TEN-MINUTE break at 8:00, the students troop *en masse* to the end of the hall for cookies, doughnuts, soda, potato chips, and even chicken soup. There is neither a delicatessen in our building nor a snack bar, but a remarkable array of vending machines stand ready to pour out their culinary blessings. A vending machine on the family farm two centuries ago would have saved our foremothers a great deal of kitchen drudgery.

The vending machine is not a modern invention, however. The ancient Greeks used a similar device to dispense holy water. In exchange for a fee, the worshiper received from his priest a small stone to be inserted into a box. The stone passed through a slot and landed on one end of a lever, causing the other end, which covered a holy-water opening, to fly up. Water drained out of the box for a moment until the stone slid off, restoring the lever to its original position.

But it is the post-World War II era that can truly be called "the Age of the Vending Machine." Even two-year-olds know that the bubble-headed machine in their supermarket will respond with gum when fed a coin.

And the variety! The machines in the university library dispense hot dogs, hamburgers, grilled cheese sandwiches, soup, stew, bananas, apples, and the usual abundance of drinks, chips, and desserts. In fact, when the library lobby was open twenty-four hours a day, some students—to avoid paying rent—brought blankets for sleeping and ate all their meals from the vending machines. They actually lived in the library lobby!

The pervasive influence of the vending economy has had spiritual repercussions. While still referring to God as a person, Christians increasingly tend to treat Him as a vending machine. If they pop in their coins of prayer, Bible study, and church attendance, He is expected to deliver "the goods": Financial security, popularity, and good health.

Observe people gathering to pray. The primary focus of this meeting will be not praise or guidance or thanksgiving, but "prayer requests."

"Does anyone have any prayer requests?"

• "Yes, I have the flu, and I'd like you to pray that God gets rid of it."

• "I'm having trouble with my car and can't afford to get it fixed, so pray that God will keep my car going."

• "We'd like you to pray that God will help us find a nice house in Omaha."

• "I'm traveling to Missouri, so pray that God will keep me safe."

I do not suggest that any of these is necessarily an illegitimate prayer or that God will refuse to answer. One of God's marvelous attributes is that He meets us where we are. Still, a consistent vending-machine mentality will likely damage our "I-Thou" relationship with God.

For one thing, we lose the feeling of gratitude. Have you ever seen anyone say "Thank you" to a vending machine? It is expected, taken for granted, that the equipment will work. When it does, the user does not exclaim in joy and appreciation; he merely goes away munching his taco chips. But when the machine fails to work, fierce is the user's vengeance! As a miniature-golf-course worker for three years, I saw people kick machines, slap them on the sides, curse them, and punch buttons desperately in a panicky attempt to get their treats or (failing that) their money back.

I have seen people curse, abuse, and verbally kick God when their expectations were not fulfilled.

"Why did He let my daughter die? I prayed about it over and over. I'll never trust Him again!"

One medical student, having done poorly on a major test, told me that if God were here on earth she'd "wring His neck"—an interesting anthropomorphism.

Other people try pushing all the buttons again: "I must have not prayed hard enough or long enough or often enough."

In every case the petitioner feels cheated by God.

Another problem with the vending-machine mentality is that it limits God's freedom of choice. I once pushed the Doublemint button on a gum machine and got a package of Juicy Fruit instead. Juicy Fruit gum, under normal conditions, is fine; but at that moment I had specifically asked for Doublemint, my appetite was whetted for Doublemint, and I expected to get Doublemint!

Despite the clear warning of Romans 8:26 that Christians often don't know what to pray for, we cling to the worldly attitude "I know what's best for me." God may feel that a period of economic insecurity or illness is vital to our maturing process, but of course we know better. If God isn't going to do it our way, He might as well not intervene at all.

A friend once asked me, "Suppose Phil [our campus minister] and another man both saw a newspaper ad for a good used-car deal, and each prayed that he would get the car. Would our campus minister win because he's a stronger Christian?" (God as game show host.) I told my friend that most likely the other man, not our campus minister, would get the car.

"Why?" my friend asked, puzzled.

"Because," I replied, "our campus minister is too mature

to back God into a corner like that. Instead he would ask God to free him from worrying about the situation and thank God for whatever blessing He intends to give."

A further difficulty with the vending-machine attitude is that it expects God to act quickly. The soda machine at the miniature golf course generally took four to five seconds to begin working—which, though long for a vending machine, is a relatively short time. Yet even in that fleeting period I saw people push the button again, push the Coin Return, and look questioningly at me to confirm that the machine was working. It was—but in its own time, not the customer's.

Similarly I have heard the Creator of Humanity, the Lord of Heaven and Earth, being asked to punch a time clock as if He were the petitioner's employee.

• "Father, if You want me to take this class, let me know this week."

• "God, I've been sick for three days. Please heal me tonight."

• "Heavenly Father, if You'll give me a job tomorrow, I'll know it's really because of You." (Notice the subtle blackmail: God cannot answer a day later, because if He does, the petitioner threatens to believe He was not involved.)

The greatest problem with the vending-machine mentality, however, is that it is guaranteed to undermine our trust in God. Both common sense and experience demonstrate that God will not answer every single request positively, just as a loving parent will not give his child candy on every request. I am sure that some of our petitions to God must seem, from His point of view, as foolish and immature as continual requests for candy.

How does this damage our relationship with God? Imagine a soda machine that delivers only 50 percent of the time. People do not gather around soda machines to admire them, to hold them, or to talk to them, but to get an "answer." If our relationship with God is based solely on the assumption that He gives us what we want, every occasion of refusal chips away at that relationship.

So should we determine not to ask God for anything? No. But in our petitions we should always follow the pattern of Christ in Gethsemane. Christ prayed fervently that He would be delivered from torture. But, realizing that His request might get in the way of God's purpose, He yielded His personal desires to God's wisdom and did physically what each of us must do mentally and emotionally: "He humbled Himself and became obedient to death; yes, death by the cross." (Philippians 2:8).

Putting Prayer Into Practice

Evaluate your relationship with God and consider whether you have fallen into the selfishness trap. Is the bulk of your prayer time given to requests? Are you often anxious for God to make your circumstances more comfortable? Ask God to give you wisdom in developing a more mature relationship with Him; decide that from now on you will be primarily concerned with pleasing Him, not yourself.

A Funny Thing Happened on the Way to Prayer Meeting

2

IT IS WEDNESDAY NIGHT, 7:35 P.M.—ALMOST TIME FOR THE 7:30 prayer meeting at Portersville Church to begin. Elders Tom Turner and Roy Cox, in an informal meeting at the back of the church, are agreed that their gardens need rain. Helen Beech, the Vacation Bible School director, is anxiously viewing the crowd in search of another possible Beginners teacher. "Crowd" is perhaps the wrong word; the usual thirty-one stalwarts are out this evening. At 7:37 the minister, Perry Koval, steps behind the carved wooden pulpit and clears his throat.

"It's about time to start," he asserts. "Let's open with a word of prayer." Mechanically the gathered saints of Portersville close their eyes and bow their heads—except, of course, for Jenny Howerton, whose two-year-old, Tony, is trying to pull a wad of aged gum from the oak pew and resurrect it in his own mouth. The gum chips off, Jenny pulls Tony away, and the opening prayer begins.

"Our Father, who art in heaven," intones the pastor, "we truly do thank Thee for this blessed privilege of prayer. Thy goodness toward us . . ."

Jenny Howerton! thought Helen Beech suddenly. *Jenny could teach the Beginners!*

17

". . . before Thy throne of grace . . ."

I forgot Tony's ball, Jenny remembers in distress. *How can I keep him quiet tonight without his favorite ball?*

". . . the many missionaries in foreign lands . . ."

I should have bought my lawn mower at Sears, Tom thought. *I didn't know they were on sale.*

". . . guide, guard, and direct us always . . ."

It's almost over, Roy mused.

"In Jesus' name, Amen."

Although to the Greeks that closing word meant "So be it," in the twentieth century it stands for "The end." Therefore the thirty-one, refreshed by intimate communication with the Lord, raise their heads and open their eyes.

"Okay," Pastor Koval begins, stepping to a chalkboard, "we're ready to take prayer requests. Does anybody have a request tonight?"

The members shift uneasily, waiting for someone to make an "appropriate" request. Helen Beech looks up. "Pastor, the Lord needs to provide a Vacation Bible School teacher for the Beginners class." She cranes her neck to see if Jenny Howerton heard that request, but Jenny is picking up the song book Tony dropped.

"Thank you, Helen." Pastor Koval carefully prints "Teacher" on the chalkboard. "Anyone else?"

"The Lord should send our gardens some rain," announces Roy Cox.

"What else?" asks Pastor Koval, writing "Rain."

"The missionaries in foreign lands," suggests Jenny Howerton. Her son Tony digs a finger in his ear, then pops it into his mouth. Jenny grimaces and pulls the offending finger away.

Everyone nods in approval of Jenny's suggestion. This is the eighty-fourth consecutive week the congregation has prayed for "missionaries in foreign lands" and they see no reason to stop now.

"That's probably enough," Pastor Koval determines,

completing the word "Missionary" on the board. "Brother Hunter, will you lead us in prayer?"

Tom Hunter's prayer lasts nearly two minutes. It is now 7:47 and time for what everyone considers the real "meat" of the evening—a lesson by the pastor on dietary laws in the Book of Leviticus.

At the turn of the century, prayer meetings were an important element of many churches. What happened to them?

In most cases they died. Television, shopping, PTA, and bowling leagues dealt critical blows. Curiously, even the people who formerly attended prayer meetings did not mourn their demise, but felt relief: It was one fewer church meeting they had to attend.

In more conservative denominations the prayer meeting has survived, usually resembling the form of the one at Portersville Church. The prayer time is centered around requests, usually perfunctory and generally falling into three categories: Sicknesses, church worker needs, and missionaries. The major portion of the prayer service is not spent in prayer, but in Bible study.

I have attended services regularly in churches of five denominations (not simultaneously). If a church member attends two hours of services (Sunday school and morning worship), no matter what the denomination, he or she will likely spend the time in this manner:

• Waiting for services to begin (eight minutes)
• Singing (twenty minutes)
• Bible study (seventy-five minutes)
• Announcements and offering (ten minutes)
• Praying (seven minutes)

The typical church spends more time listening to announcements than it does praying.

But, one might argue, the quality of the time spent praying is more important than the quantity. That argument is weak—Can a concert pianist succeed with ten minutes of "quality" practice time per week?—but let us grant it. What is the quality of our typical congregation's prayer time?

Abominable. The Sunday school lesson "opens" and "closes" with prayer; the words indicate a way of marking time rather than an act of adoration or a conversation with God. Similarly the worship service opens and closes with ritualistic prayers; in between are prayers for the congregation (long) and the offering (short). Members of the church do not pray aloud, ever. They listen to a minister or elder pray. He determines both the amount of time spent in prayer and the subjects to be covered.

To illustrate the problem with this approach suppose you have been invited to a neighbor's house to meet the president of the United States personally. You are tremendously excited, of course, along with the twenty other people in the room. When the president enters, however, he is not allowed by your neighbor to speak, nor are any of you allowed to speak to him. Instead the neighbor speaks briefly to the president on your behalf, then delivers an hour lecture on the president's life. As you leave in disappointment, the neighbor invites you to return the following week to hear another lecture on the president's life.

"But will I not be allowed to speak to the president myself?" you ask in amazement.

"Certainly, if you make arrangements of your own," the neighbor replies. "But in my house, you'll have to be satisfied with hearing *me* talk to him."

"Couldn't we listen to the president speak for himself?" you ask.

"Absolutely not!" the neighbor replies. "That would make our gathering much less orderly. And besides"—he mutters in a low voice—"each of you would then be as important as I." Bidding the neighbor good-night, you realize your chances of getting to know the president personally are dim.

Without being overly anthropomorphic, I think we can understand from this why Christians often find it difficult or uncomfortable to pray. We are not taught how, nor are we given opportunities to learn or to practice with others.

But times are changing. Since the publication of the book *Prayer: Conversing with God* by Rosalind Rinker in 1959,[1] small prayer groups in the United States have burgeoned. And now that people have started to pray together, they are asking questions about prayer. Fortunately, the New Testament has answers.

Putting Prayer Into Practice

1. What percentage of time does your church spend in prayer? Can you think of ways to make that time more meaningful?

2. Can you find a person (spouse, neighbor, business associate, church friend) with whom to pray occasionally? Think of that person now and ask God to give you courage to raise the subject. You might want to mention to her that you are reading a book on prayer and wish to try out some ideas.

3. Is there a prayer group in the church or neighborhood you can join? If not, can you think of three or four individuals or couples who might be interested?

4. Will you right now—before reading another chapter —make a personal commitment to God to spend regular time in prayer with Him?

[1](Grand Rapids: Zondervan, 1959).

"Come, Lord Jesus, Be Our Guest"

3

SOME PEOPLE, PERHAPS, CAN DRIVE RIGHT PAST A SIGN THAT AD-
vertises 3 TACOS FOR $1. Audrey and I can't. So on the
way home from church one day, our previous lunch plans
were scrapped and I wheeled our 1971 Volkswagen into the
Taco-Tico parking lot.

"Six tacos, mild sauce," I requested and was about to add,
"for here," when a voice boomed behind me.

"Well, look who's joining the fast-food crowd today! You
always have an eye out for a taco special, don't you?"

I turned to see two good friends from church, Kenny and
Twila Pound, grinning in delight. We expressed our mutual
admiration for tacos and for the morning sermon, then I
carried the lunch tray out to the booth where Audrey was
waiting. She and I each unwrapped a taco, then did a curious,
unusual thing.

We prayed.

Praying in a restaurant is unusual enough in itself, but even
more so for Audrey and me. We *never* pray in restaurants.
Yet, on this day we simultaneously felt an urge to pray, and
each of us bent over our trays and blessed the tacos. When we
finished our prayers, Audrey and I opened our eyes and

looked at each other. Both of us flushed in shame upon realizing what had just happened.

Our prayers were sins against God.

That seems odd, doesn't it? If we had eaten our lunch as usual, all would have been well; but by stopping to pray, we both committed sin. When Audrey and I looked at each other, we knew that our prayers had not been directed toward God, but toward Kenny and Twila. We felt sure that, being a religious couple, they would pray for their food; what would they think if we didn't?

There is nothing inherently holy about the act of prayer itself. This surprises most people, especially non-Christians, who think of eating, sex, and exercise as "natural" acts, while prayer, Bible study, and church attendance are "spiritual" acts. As Brother Lawrence observed, however, even mundane acts like gardening can be done in a worshipful attitude.

By contrast, a person may engage in an "act of worship" for a wrong reason. Suppose a church member combs her Bible in order to humiliate a Sunday school teacher who has erred regarding the exact age of Methusaleh. Or another, expecting the pastor to call at 4:00, begins studying the Scriptures at 3:55 in order to greet him with Bible in hand. St. Augustine wrote that God created all things good, but they can be perverted into evil. That includes prayer.

Christ warns His disciples against one perversion of prayer in Matthew 6:5–6. Five other verses in the chapter—"the Lord's Prayer"—are probably the best known in the Bible, but the earlier verses relate why that prayer was given.

> *"And when you pray, do not be like the hypocrites; for they love to pray standing in the synagogues and at the street corners to be seen by the people. I assure you, they have been paid in full. But you, when you pray, enter your inner room and with your door closed pray to your Father who is there in the secret place, and your Father who sees in secret will reward you" (Matthew 6:5–6).*

Jesus attacks here a misunderstanding of prayer—the ritualistic, hypocritical attitude that prayer is an activity to be performed merely to look religious. But, one may object, certainly few people have the hypocritical attitude of the Pharisees today; we pray because we mean it, not because we are supposed to do so.

Perhaps. Yet it seems to me that Christians have bound prayer to certain activities so often that it becomes a ritual rather than a meaningful attempt to know God. Why do we always pray before each act of eating, but not before each act of bathing, lovemaking, television watching, or cooking? Is the act of eating more sacred than cooking or doing the dishes? We have made a mere habit of prayer.

Some habits are good, of course. I habitually try to rinse out the bathtub after showering in order to please my wife. But the rinsing of the tub is not a meaningful act in itself; it is important only as an expression of love. Aristotle observed that people naturally tend to confuse means and ends, and the longer an act continues, the more likely it is to become an end. Imagine this dialogue taking place between my wife and me:

Audrey: Marv, could you come quick? There's a chipmunk in our yard.

Me: I can't. I'm rinsing out the tub.

Audrey: Oh, please hurry! I'm afraid he's going to leave.

Me: Look, I'm supposed to keep things clean around here! That's what you want, and that's what I intend to do.

A "magic moment" in our marriage is lost because I have forgotten the love behind the act of love. Similarly, when prayer becomes the "introduction" to a meal—the signal to begin eating—it may cease to be prayer.

Now, I assuredly favor recognizing God as the Provider. Jesus prayed before He fed the five thousand (Matthew 14:19). My point is that those meal prayers, when offered, should be taken seriously. Our family sometimes prays at the end of a meal—my four-year-old's concentration is better then!—and sometimes we sing a hymn of thanks. We pray at four or five meals each week.

I would not accomplish my purpose by causing you merely to pray fewer (but more meaningful) prayers at mealtime. The question is, Around what other activities can we develop a closer relationship with God? The answer, of course, is "virtually everything."

In college I began the practice of singing the Doxology ("Praise God, From Whom All Blessings Flow") every time my car survived another ten thousand miles. It isn't a heavy obligation—I feel no guilt if I should miss the "big moment"—but a delightful time of praise and gratitude. My last car made it to 137,000 miles and the current one has 129,000 miles, so I have had many opportunities to praise God!

On the next page I suggest some activities to consider as moments for praise. But I want you to be creative and determine some of your own. For instance, even though I don't list brushing teeth, it would be a delight to God for you to pause occasionally before brushing, look in the mirror, and thank God for those marvelously efficient grinders and your smile. (Yes, you can celebrate dentures, too!)

As we noted in chapter 2, church services often contain prayers of the "mealtime" variety. If you have some influence on the order of worship in your congregation, use it to make prayer less ritualistic and more worshipful. The offering prayer, for example, can be a psalm of praise from the Bible, or it can be omitted and God thanked for the words of one of the morning hymns instead. Rather than a formal closing prayer at the end of a Sunday school class, the hour can end with a few minutes of small group prayers, perhaps applying the teachings of the lesson.

Can you thank God for the exercise you get while cutting the grass tomorrow?

Putting Prayer Into Practice

1. Mealtime prayers can come not only before, but also after and even during a meal. ("During" means after the main

courses and before dessert.) Why not take turns around the table, each person thanking God for a different food or a different part of the meal's preparation? Or—I recommend this highly—each person can thank God for a different event or experience during the day.

2. Can you schedule regular times of praise for God in other matters? You could celebrate, either individually or as a family, each new crop from the garden, each good book read, and exceptionally good TV shows. Make a list of several activities you do regularly, from shutting off the alarm each morning to collapsing in the bed each night, and put it on the refrigerator or bulletin board. Try to "pause for praise" at a different activity each day. Change the list every month or so.

Teach Us
to Pray

4

SOMEONE HAS OBSERVED THAT WHEN JESUS' DISCIPLES WERE
ready to begin their ministries, they did not come to Him and
say, "Lord, teach us to preach." Neither did they ask for
advice in building construction, in counseling, or even in that
crucial modern task, increasing the offering. They simply
requested, "Lord, teach us to pray" (Luke 11:1).

Christ instructed them with the Lord's Prayer. But first He
had to erase two misconceptions: The Jewish concept of
prayer as a religious activity (discussed in chapter 3), and the
pagan concept of prayer as a method of bullying God (or the
gods) into compliance. Jesus said of repetition,

> "When you pray do not repeat and repeat as the pagans do; for they
> imagine that for their much talking they will secure a hearing. Do not
> be like them, for your Father knows your need before you ask Him.
> This, then, is the way you should pray:
>
> "Our Father who art in heaven, Thy name be kept holy. Thy
> kingdom come, Thy will be done on earth as in heaven.
>
> "Give us today our daily bread. And forgive us our debts as we have
> forgiven our debtors. And lead us not into temptation but deliver us
> from the evil one" (Matthew 6:7–13).

When missionaries began to penetrate the Far East, they were
often amazed at finding "prayer wheels" among the people.

The wheels came in a variety of types, but most commonly they were wind or water driven and had places to attach written prayers. When a person had a particularly urgent prayer to make, he could affix it to a paddle; each time the paddle went round, another petition was offered to heaven.

The prayer wheel is a concept that many Americans would simply laugh at. But I believe Christ's teaching on repetition stretches beyond the primitives to include our own efforts. Contemporary confusion over how to pray is well illustrated by an incident that occurred nearly 900 years earlier. First Kings 18 tells of a contest between Elijah and the prophets of Baal to see whose God was stronger. Elijah proposed that each side slaughter a bull and lay it on an altar, but not set fire to the wood. The prophets of Baal agreed to the match, killed a bull, and began to pray.

> So they took the bullock he gave them, prepared it, and called upon the name of Baal from morning until noon, saying, "O Baal, hear us!" but there was no sound or response. They hopped about the altar they had made. About noon Elijah began to taunt them, "Shout louder, for he is a god; he is in conversation or he has gone out; he is on a trip; or perhaps he is asleep and must be awakened." So they shouted more loudly and cut themselves with swords and lances, as they were accustomed to do, until the blood ran out over them. After noon they continued to rave until the time for the evening sacrifice; but there was no sound, no answer, no recognition (1 Kings 18:26–29).

Then Elijah took his turn.

> At the time for the evening sacrifice, Elijah the prophet came up and said, "O LORD, God of Abraham, Isaac, and Israel, today let it be known that Thou art God in Israel, that I am Thy servant, and that I have done all this in accordance with Thy word. Hear me, O LORD, hear me, that this people may see that Thou, O LORD, art God and that Thou hast turned their hearts back again" (vv. 36–37).

One can see how little the prophets of Baal respected their deity. For a full eight-hour day (plus overtime), they cajoled and pleaded. As the prayers went unanswered, they became frenzied, almost maniacal. What a contrast it must have been as evening neared and Elijah stepped over their panting, bleeding bodies to his altar! He calmly uttered two sentences, full of faith, and fire sprang down from heaven.

What does this have to do with us, who use neither knives nor prayer wheels? When Jesus cautions against repetition, He is concerned with the motivation behind it. Clearly, Jesus does not mean that it is sinful for me to praise for a certain blessing today and to repeat that prayer tomorrow; but it is wrong for me to feel that by badgering God with repeated pleas I can change His mind.

When my son turned three years old, two new events occurred in our home. He began to be afraid of the dark. For several nights in a row, Rocky made the same quavery comment: "Daddy, I'm scared. Will you pray for me?" We would ask God to calm Rocky down, and Rocky would peacefully slide under the covers.

At the same age, Rocky discovered the ice cream bicycles that roam our streets. This child, who sometimes cannot hear a point-blank request to put his shoes on, has a range of about three blocks when it comes to hearing the ice cream bell.

"Daddy, can I have a 'Superstar'?" ("Superstars" are red-white-and-blue popsicles.)

"No, you may not."

"But I want one."

"I know, but you can't have one."

"Can I have an ice cream sandwich?"

His continuing hope is that if I don't give in to the first request, perhaps I will to the second or the third or—if I would allow that many—the thirteenth.

I never minded Rocky's requests for nighttime reassurance, but the ice cream requests were a different story. I suspect our prayer relationship with God is sometimes as immature as Rocky's repeated pleadings for ice cream. We ask God on Monday for someone to make an offer on the car we're trying to sell. If nothing happens, we remind God on

Tuesday, Wednesday, and Thursday. By Friday, then, we are panicky. "Why won't God answer me? Doesn't He know I need the money?"

At this point prayer tends to become more emotional. "Lord, *please* help me sell that car! I *have* to have the money! *Please* help me sell it!" Like the prophets of Baal, we are letting our blood flow (verbally) to convince God of our earnestness.

I am not necessarily against emotionalism during prayer. Like many other Christians, I have occasionally wept over a new realization of God's love or forgiveness. But I do reject the belief that by being emotional or repetitious, we'll convince God we really do need what we're asking for.

In a recent letter I mentioned to a friend that I am currently between jobs. She wrote back, "Your future paychecks are among my prayer items, but not a high priority, because I know you will get a job." If ever a sentence caught the typical evangelical attitude toward prayer, that's it. She has written what most of us feel inside—that for ordinary problems we can pray calmly once or twice, but for major matters we need to pray over and over again, sometimes emotionally. Yet, by believing this we imply that God is either not good enough to fulfill our needs and desires or not wise enough to know them. Jesus pointed out that God knows what we need even before we ask.

Two questions remain to be answered. One—"Didn't Jesus teach persistent prayer in parables?"—will be discussed in the next chapter. The second is, "If God knows all our needs before we ask, what's the use of asking Him for anything?" The key phrase there is, "What's the use?"

When I taught English to high school freshmen, they could usually see the benefits of learning to write more clearly. After all, the business world is full of memos, reports, letters, and resumes. Whenever we started a literature unit, however, they always wondered about its utility in the "real world."

"How will knowing Shakespeare help us get a job?" they would ask. I could talk about understanding other people's attitudes and actions better, about appreciation of beauty, about illustrations of moral dangers and virtues; but because of our society's economic orientation, many of them never understood those values. "I can't make more money by knowing how to read poetry."

Similarly most of us want our prayers to have a "use." If asking God for things is not going to make our lives more pleasant and comfortable, why bother?

This is the deepest misconception about prayer in the current evangelical community, so I emphasize the answer. *Prayer requests for physical needs are not made simply to receive the objects, but primarily to acknowledge the sovereignty of God.*

Let me illustrate the concept this way: As a teenager living at home I was allowed to use one of the family cars whenever I wished. If Mom and Dad were not home when I needed it, I simply took it. But if they were home, I would go to Dad and say, "Dad, I have a basketball game uptown tonight. May I use the car?" To a casual observer who did not understand the situation, it would have appeared that my primary motivation for asking was to gain use of the car. But *I could have had the car without asking.* My primary reason for requesting it was to recognize Dad as the provider, to let him know that I knew it came from him.

In Jesus' example of prayer—the Lord's Prayer—the physical request is "Give us today our daily bread." Besides its literal meaning, "bread" stands for our other physical necessities also. The disciples could look around and see that a refusal to pray did not cause starvation. Prayer is not simply a magic wand to fill larders, then, but a humble bow toward the Source of all the world's provisions. If you ask God for a safe trip to work tomorrow and your neighbor does not, it is very likely that both of you will arrive safely anyway. But only one of you will be properly grateful.

The words that close Matthew 6 are indicative of a Christian's proper mental attitude. Few people have realized this includes our attitude during prayer.

> *"Do not, then, be anxious, saying, 'What shall we eat?' or 'What shall we drink?' or 'What are we to wear?' For on all these things pagans center their interest while your heavenly Father knows that you need them all. But you, seek first His kingdom and His righteousness and all these things will be added to you" (Matthew 6:31–33).*

Putting Prayer Into Practice

1. It is difficult to make requests for the primary purpose of glorifying God rather than improving our circumstances. One way of breaking this pattern is to switch prayer requests with a close friend or relative (such as a roommate, spouse, or prayer-group associate). Meet with this person once a week for several weeks and exchange any problems troubling you. Then, during your prayers the following week, make your personal requests known to God briefly, but concentrate more fully on discussing with God your partner's needs. If God answers the prayers positively, you will rejoice in His power, not just in the improved circumstances.

2. "Apply your mind to things above, not to things on earth" (Colossians 3:2). For which do you pray more eagerly: Meekness or recovery from illness? Faith or a new job? (I'm the same way; I've never desired patience and gentleness as desperately as I've desired relief from a migraine.) As you read through the New Testament and other religious works, look for spiritual attitudes and values displayed by Christ and the apostles. Start your prayers with requests for these qualities.

The Most Misunderstood Parable in the Bible

5

BRENDA'S PARENTS HAD JUST DIVORCED, AND SHE WAS DISCON-solate. Nothing could bring them back together, she thought, until she heard the Sunday morning sermon. The minister was preaching on a parable from the Gospel of Luke, and he pointed out that by persistent prayer you can receive whatever you want.

This was welcome news to Brenda. As a child she had often pestered her parents about toys until they gave in, but she had never realized she was supposed to do that with God. The minister even implied that God is disappointed with people who only ask once; He apparently enjoys irritating insistence.

Brenda made up her mind to pray about the divorce until God simply had to answer, tired of hearing the same prayer over and over. She prayed, believing, for almost a month. After all, didn't the Bible say this was what God wanted?

Brenda is now resigned to the permanent separation of her parents. She did learn something from her experience: Never to trust God for anything again.

The parable causing her consternation occurs in Luke 11:5–13. Unlike most parables, it has no settled name, so I will call it the Parable of the Midnight Friend. According to

Luke, Jesus had just taught His disciples the model prayer; then He "further said to them" the parable.

> *"Let us say that one of you has a friend to whom he goes at midnight and says, 'Friend, lend me three loaves of bread, since a friend of mine has arrived at my house from a trip and I have nothing to set before him,' and the one inside should answer him, 'Do not bother me. The door is already locked and my children are in bed with me. I cannot get up and give to you.'*
>
> *"I tell you, if he does not get up to give to him because he is his friend, he will rise on account of his brazen insistence, and give him as much as he needs. And I tell you, Ask, and it will be given you; seek, and you will find; knock, and it will be opened to you; for everyone who asks receives, everyone who seeks finds, and to everyone who knocks the door will be opened. What father among you whose son requests a fish will instead hand him a snake, or if he requests an egg will hand him a scorpion? If you then, evil as you are, know enough to give good gifts to your children, how much more will the heavenly Father give the Holy Spirit to those who ask Him"* (Luke 11:5–13).

This passage is repeatedly cited to assert that people should be persistent in their requests to God. According to this argument, God is the householder and we as petitioners are the midnight friend. I do not argue here against petitionary prayer in general; but I am persuaded that this parable fails to support *repetitive* petitionary prayer. In fact, I think the story actually strikes against repetition.

Consider some of the difficulties in equating ourselves with the friend and God with the householder. First, the friend asks the householder to "lend" the loaves of bread, thereby implying he would pay them back. How can this illustrate our dependency on God? In the model prayer, Jesus more fittingly said, "Give us today our daily bread," not "Loan us a loaf of bread today, and we will pay You back tomorrow."

Second, the friend bothers the householder at an inconvenient time. Had the situation occurred at noon, the householder might well have granted the request more quickly.

Clearly this is a distinction from God, who lives beyond time and can never be inconvenienced.

Also, the two men pictured here are merely friends, whereas our relationship with God is much stronger, that of Father and son or daughter. Jesus clarifies this point in His comments that follow the parable.

Moreover, the "brazen insistence" of the friend can hardly be considered a Christian virtue to imitate. According to a footnote in *The Berkeley Version,* the Greek word *anaideia* could as easily be translated "shamelessness" or "impudence." Indeed, R. C. H. Lenski's commentary on the Gospel of Luke translates it "shamelessness." While we are to approach God without trembling, surely He does not wish to be greeted with impudence.

Finally, the householder's character differs from God's in two important ways. The householder displays a selfish, irritated attitude. God may answer some petitions with "No" or "Later," but He would never reply, "Do not bother Me."

Equally noticeable is the householder's change of mind. He grants the request solely because of nagging; the claim of friendship had no appeal. To impute his attitude to God would be inconceivable: God would not be touched by our relationship with Him as children, but by our shameless persistence. If that were true, a pagan could receive his desires from God as readily as a Christian. (Even more readily, because the pagan would have less hesitation about being impudent to the Father!) Besides, God is the "Father of Lights, with whom no variation occurs nor shadow cast by turning" (James 1:17), a proclamation declared in the context of God's generosity.

The verbs *ask, seek,* and *knock* are iteratives, which means they refer to a repeated action: "Continually seek, and you will find." This implies persistence; but when this is taken—as it often is—to be persistent after a particular desire, I feel the emphasis is misplaced. While the grammar allows this interpretation, it can also mean—and likely does—that we are to continually ask God in all matters of life. In other words, God is not bothered (as the householder certainly would be) if we ask Him for something today after having made requests yesterday. Despite having sought forgiveness for yesterday's sins, I may still approach God with today's failures. As verse 10 states, "The door will be opened."

Jesus drives home His point by illustrating the difference between a father and the householder. The questions are obviously rhetorical. No fathers—particularly in the closely knit Jewish families to whom He was speaking—would mistreat their sons in that way.

The questions serve Jesus' purpose brilliantly, because they point out the fathers' refusal to give a foolish or harmful gift, but do not tell what gift is actually given. Perhaps those men might well have been thinking this: "If it were my son hungry and asking for a fish, I'd give him a fish. Why, I'd give him three or four fish, and bread to go with them. If he were hungry and asked for an egg, I'd give him eggs, and rice as well."

Jesus' questions were designed to make those fathers think about what they actually would give their hungry sons. The fathers' natural generosity would compel them to give beyond the sons' simple request for one egg or one fish. In thinking on this passage, I recall how my own father always allowed his children to have the best cuts of meat, unselfishly chewing on the tougher ones himself.

To make sure the fathers don't miss the point, Jesus connects their own unselfish impulses with God's. "Evil as you are," He explains, "you know enough to give good gifts to your children. How much more will the heavenly Father give the Holy Spirit to those who ask Him?"

As eager as the earthly fathers are to give good gifts to their children, despite being tainted by innate selfishness, God is much more eager to satisfy His children. And because He is God, He gives not just a good gift, but the best of gifts: The Holy Spirit. This is clearly not a reluctant householder, but a loving, eager, rich, all-wise Father who gives His children beyond what they deserve or even ask for.

Why is this parable continually twisted in the meaning given to it? Probably it's because, after twenty centuries, we still have so much trouble accepting the idea of Grace as unmerited favor. As American Christians, imbued with the work ethic, we are naturally suspicious of "something for nothing." This is true not only of salvation ("good enough to get to heaven"), but also of prayer.

Somehow praying to God for a concern and waiting patiently and thankfully for His answer seems too easy. We feel that by constantly wrestling with God and keeping the problem before Him we have "earned" the right to be heard.

The detrimental effect of this parable's misinterpretation should be apparent. Instead of exercising faith in God, we place our faith in the effort. To properly explain this parable requires not only a distinction between God and the householder, but also a similar distinction between "earning" prayer answers and receiving them freely. God grants requests, not through compulsion, but through love.

Putting Prayer Into Practice

. Repeated requests for reassurance show a lack of trust. It is like saying to one's spouse, "Are you sure you'll pick me up at four o'clock? Are you positive? You won't forget, will you? Are you really sure?" Sometimes when we are particularly worried we may need that constant reassurance, but it is not an attitude calculated to endear a person to his spouse. Ask God to increase your faith in Him, in the fact that no matter what happens, even if it hurts, He always wants the best for you.

Do You Get What You Pray For?

6

"AND EVERYTHING YOU ASK IN PRAYER YOU WILL OBTAIN IF YOU believe" (Matthew 21:22). Some passages of Scripture seem almost to invite misapplication and confusion. A boy died in Missouri. Claiming this promise of Christ, the parents refused to bury their son, but instead kept him in a deep freeze for nearly a week while they prayed for his resurrection. The young man was not resurrected, of course, so the family finally consented to his burial.

Certainly the verse in Matthew does not apply directly to us in the sense we would expect. Both experience and Scripture deny that. The apostle Paul, a man beside whom our faith appears minute, prayed fervently that God would remove his famous "thorn in the flesh." (Traditionally writers pause to speculate on what that mysterious thorn was; but I really don't care. Sorry.) God did not remove it from Paul. In the same way, anyone who has been a Christian for very long has had the experience of praying for something and not receiving it.[1]

The exact meaning of the passage is perhaps unexplainable

---

[1]There is an excellent discussion of this problem in chapter 14 of Joni Eareckson and Steve Estes's book on Christian faith and suffering, *A Step Further* (Grand Rapids: Zondervan, 1978).

this side of heaven. It has baffled everyone from the early church fathers to C. S. Lewis. To me a more crucial question is "Do we want what we pray for?"

Often in our prayers we seem to be in the position of advising God. Some of His options might be distasteful or uncomfortable for us, so we narrow down those options. We pray for God to give us a specific thing we desire, reasoning that He can't give us anything different or He would be going back on His promise in Matthew 21:22.

Our family had just moved to a new city, and we were engaged in the traditional pastime of "church shopping." We took some Sunday school literature from most of the congregations we visited. In one junior magazine, the lead story told of a boy so poor he did not have a winter coat. (I wonder how well the middle-class kids in this suburban congregation identified with him.) The boy was told by his mother to pray about it—advice with which I have no quarrel. But then she told him to tell God exactly what kind of coat he wanted. The boy "put in his order" with God for a brown coat, knee-length, with fur trim. (I almost titled this book *God Is Not a Sears Roebuck Catalog.*) When no coat magically appeared, the boy assumed God wasn't going to answer.

That afternoon our hero was invited to a neighbor's house to play. As he was leaving, the neighbor's mother said, "Johnny, my Freddie has outgrown his coat from last year. Would you like to try it on?" Since God had apparently not come through, Johnny was quite willing to settle for a lesser coat. But when Freddie's mother brought out the coat, can you guess what color it was? (That's right.) And what length? (Right again.) And what trim? (Bingo!) Now little Johnny knew that God did answer prayer, because He had tailored the coat to Johnny's specifications.

The frequency of specific prayers has grown immensely since the publication of Rosalind Rinker's book *Prayer: Conversing With God.* Rinker recommends specific prayer as a way of showing that God does answer prayer. I certainly agree with her in the need to avoid vague platitudes: "Bless all the sick and ill of our congregation." (Whenever I hear that prayer, I can't help wondering what the difference is between the sick and the ill.) When we make a specific request, indeed we can sometimes see the working of God.

For example, I was asked to travel to the airport in Dayton, Ohio, to meet a speaker for Ball State University. I am always anxious to have the guidance of the Holy Spirit in sharing Christ, so on the way to Dayton I prayed that if the Holy Spirit wanted me to share Christ with the speaker, He would cause the speaker to ask what church congregation I attended. Sure enough, about five miles away from the airport she asked me that very question. She was, as it turned out, hungrier to hear about Christ than anyone else I had ever met.

I believe, therefore, in the value of specific prayer. Yet too often people assume that the concept of specific prayer means laying out all the details for God.

Some friends in our congregation showed us through a home they had bought upon moving to our town. As we examined the study, the wife explained, "We prayed for a room like this. We also prayed for a house with two stories." As we toured the house, the couple appeared to have prayed also for a blue interior and a basement. The clincher, though, came in the kitchen.

Elaine pointed out the prayed-for kitchen appliances, which were the correct color, and then pointed across the room. "Now look at this," she said, beaming. "A dishwasher! We didn't even pray for that. God just threw it in as an extra!"

If there is anything the New Testament teaches it is that God is wiser than we are. The key text affirming this is Romans 8:26: "In a similar way the Spirit joins in to help us in our weakness; for we do not know what and how we ought to pray, but the Spirit Himself intercedes on our behalf with sighs too deep for words."

St. Augustine's life provides an apt example of this truth. As a young man, an agnostic, Augustine announced to his devout mother his intention of going to Rome. At the time, Rome's reputation paralleled that of modern Hollywood: A mecca of sexual immorality, drunkenness, and iniquity. Augustine's mother, Monica, was understandably horrified. (My own mother felt the same way when she discovered I was going to attend the University of Missouri.)

Fearing that Rome would pull Augustine permanently into moral decay, Monica prayed that God would keep him from boarding the ship. In his *Confessions,* Augustine describes the situation: "And what, O Lord, was she with so many tears asking of You, but that You would not allow me to sail? But You, in the depth of Your counsels, and *hearing the main point of her desire, regarded not what she then asked, that You might make me what she always asked.*"[2] In other words, God knew that the primary concern of Monica's prayers was not the ship, but Augustine's salvation.

Suppose that God had granted Monica's request about Augustine's not boarding the boat. He would have delayed Augustine's conversion to Christianity!

Could we stand living in a world where requests were automatically granted, where our wisdom was allowed to overrule God's? Mark Twain hypothesizes this situation in chapter 7 of *The Mysterious Stranger.* An angel has revealed to young Theodor Fischer that a girl named Lisa Brandt will die in twelve days. When Theodor wonders why the angel will not guard her from death, the angel shows what the rest of her life would be.

> ". . . *ten years of pain and slow recovery from an accident, and then . . . nineteen years' pollution, shame, depravity, crime, ending with death at the hands of the executioner. Twelve days hence she will die; her mother would save her life if she could. Am I not kinder than her mother?*"
>
> "*Yes—oh, indeed yes, and wiser.*"

[2]My modern rendering of Edward Pusey's translation, from book V.

44

"We do not know what and how we ought to pray. . . ." This sentence has profound implications for our prayers. Why should we attempt to pin God down to a lesser blessing than He may desire for us? Does not Scripture teach that the foolishness of God is wiser than the wisdom of people? I take God's "foolishness" to be those acts of His which we find uncomfortable or displeasing, but which are for our real good. Limiting my four-year-old to three desserts a week is better than allowing unlimited sweets; but Rocky, of course, thinks I merely want to thwart his pleasure. He considers my limits foolishness.

In difficult circumstances, then—such as illness, unemployment, or depression—how can we pray? We have two positive choices. On the one hand, we can honestly tell God what we want, but then commit ourselves to accepting His will without complaining. This is what Christ did in Gethsemane, where He expressed His desire to avoid the cross but bravely committed Himself to the will of His Father (Matthew 26:39–44).

On the other hand, we can pray for spiritual strength in the situation, the ability to learn and mature from our circumstances. Apparently that is what Paul and Silas did when they were in jail at Philippi. They were so filled with joy that they were still singing hymns at midnight (Acts 16:24–25).

A woman in our prayer group taught me a significant lesson. After mentioning an illness she had had for several weeks, she said, "Last week was the first time I've been able to praise God for it. You see, ever since childhood I've had terrible eating habits. I kept asking God to take this illness away, but last week I realized that perhaps He is allowing my sickness to help me see my eating problem. I've started paying attention to health for the first time, and I'm so glad God let me learn from my sickness."

It might seem hard—perhaps impossible—to tell a suffering cancer victim praying for recovery that she must let her utmost desire be to patiently accept God's will, even if that includes more suffering. But this same God said, "Love your enemies, bless those who curse you." He is not the God of the Easy.

Putting Prayer Into Practice

1. Perhaps in suffering or anxiety you cannot yet honestly tell God that you want His will most of all. Try to manage a prayer like this: "Please, dear Father, please make me well. I love You whether You do or not, but I feel as if I can't bear this pain any longer. Please help me—I know You can; but even if you decide not to, I love and adore You anyway."

2. In John 9:3, Jesus said a man was born blind that "God's works should be displayed." You can also use an unpleasant situation to glorify God. Ask Him to help you display joy, patience, gentleness, or another attribute from Galatians 5:22—23 in a specific way, such as caressing a child who has been on your nerves.

Changes in Attitude

7

"MY PH.D. COMPREHENSIVE EXAMS ARE NEXT WEEK. IF I DON'T pass them, I won't get my degree."

"Are you worried?"

"No, not a bit. I'm just going to do my best."

"Yes, I know what you mean. Our farm crops haven't had rain for six weeks, but I'm not overly concerned."

"Me either, even though we can't pay my wife's medical bills from this spring and the boss said I might get laid off."

"I understand. My doctor thinks I have cancer, but he won't know until next week. It'll be interesting to find out the diagnosis, but I can wait."

If you can picture yourself taking part in this conversation, two things are clear: (1) You can skip this chapter; (2) You're not human.

Almost everyone worries. It seems as natural to worry as to eat, sleep, or breathe. There is, however, one major difference between worrying and these other activities: Worry is detrimental to our health.

The book *None of These Diseases* indicates God's marvelous provision for His people in ways they never understood.[1]

---

[1] S. I. McMillen (Old Tappan, N.J.: Fleming H. Revell, 1963).

The restriction against pork, for example, saved the Israelites from trichinosis. The circumcision requirement reduced the incidence of cancer of the cervix among women. Similarly, during the past century God's wisdom in forbidding worry and continual, smoldering anger has been more fully appreciated as modern psychology has informed us of their destructive consequences.

"But I pray, and I still worry," you may say. "Why is that?" A study on the subject offers some helpful answers to this question.

A large group of people suffering emotional depression was divided into four smaller groups. The members of the first small group were asked to pray about their problems every day for a month. The people in the second group were given regular counseling for a month. The subjects of the third were taught to turn problems over to God as they arose and then not to pray about those particular problems again. The fourth group, a control group, was simply asked to continue normal activities.

At the end of the month the control group, as expected, showed little change. Some members improved emotionally; others declined. Of the subjects given counseling (group 2), some improved; a few declined; the majority stayed the same. The majority of those who had been taught how to pray (group 3) improved, although a few remained the same. The major surprise, however, was the condition of those who had prayed about their problems for a month (group 1). *The emotional condition of those who prayed about their problems daily almost universally declined.*

This study suggests that while prayer can be beneficial in reducing anxiety, it is not a panacea or cure-all. The blessings of prayer are due not to the prayer itself, but to the omnipotent Creator receiving the prayer. Too often we fool ourselves into thinking we are praying when we are actually griping to God.

How do we go about "throwing all our anxiety on Him"

in prayer (1 Peter 5:7)? The fullest answer is found in Philippians 4:4–9.

> Be joyful in the Lord always; again I say, Rejoice. Be known by all the people for your considerateness; the Lord is near. Entertain no worry, but under all circumstances let your petitions be made known before God by prayer and pleading along with thanksgiving. So will the peace of God, that surpasses all understanding, keep guard over your hearts and your thoughts in Christ Jesus.
>
> Finally, brothers, whatever is true, whatever is honorable, whatever is just, whatever is pure, whatever is lovely, whatever is kindly spoken, whatever is lofty and whatever is praiseworthy—put your mind on these. And what you have learned and received and heard and seen in me, that put into practice. And the God of peace will be with you.

The word "entertain" in this translation arouses interest, doesn't it? It sounds as though we ask worry to "make itself at home" in our minds. Worry is not a permanent part of our mental environment; it can be asked to leave.

In fact, as "under all circumstances" indicates, the middle of this section offers a pattern for virtually every request we make of God. We pray pleadingly; we give thanks; we accept His peace even though we don't understand what God is doing.

Unfortunately, even though we have to invite worry into our minds at first, like an imperious guest it has a way of coming back uninvited again and again. This is why even though the day before your visit to the dentist you decided absolutely not to worry about it again, you woke up the next morning with your stomach churning. What we need, obviously, is a guard to protect our thoughts from that intruder, Worry. Behold (to use a King James word), that is exactly what we are promised here.

Like many other aspects of the Christian life, this one blends the sovereignty of God and our free will. Since worry has been evicted from our mental house, we now have an obligation to entertain other guests, eight of which are listed here in Philippians.

It seems clear that if we spend a great deal of our prayer time—and spare time—meditating on the pure and lofty, we will spend less time being anxious. But have you ever tried to meditate on Paul's suggestions as abstract concepts? Can you imagine spending ten minutes thinking abstractly about justice, purity, and loveliness?

Paul couldn't. He instructs us to put our minds not on the general—"Truth"; but on the specific—"Whatever is true." There are four ways we can give flesh to these abstract bones: We can meditate on these qualities in God's scriptural action, God's personal action, the lives of distant saints, and the lives of local saints.

1. God's scriptural action. As we read the Bible, we encounter vivid illustrations that God possesses the holy qualities mentioned in Philippians 4. Consider, for example, Christ's conversation with the woman at the well (John 4). The woman had lived with six different men, and we can assume it would have been quite natural for a stranger to look at her leeringly or lustfully. She probably conveyed sensuality. Christ, however, kept His attention strictly focused on the woman's needs; His personal purity is striking. Similarly, when we read of the evil in Sodom and Gomorrah (Genesis 19), it is easy to appreciate God's justice in making sure those people were destroyed.

When reading sections like this that reveal God's attributes, we can put the Bible aside a few minutes and meditate on God's goodness. Or, if we wish, we can jot down the thought and return to it in our prayer time later in the day.

2. God's personal action. We can reflect on ways in which God has improved our lives, what He has done for us. It may be that we have received a compliment about something. (We have been "kindly spoken.") We should take the time, either then or later, to thank God for it. Besides guarding our minds from worry, it also guards our humility to remember that all of our compliments should be privately passed on to God.

Remember our car with 129,000 miles from chapter 3?

Audrey and I decided it had reached the mandatory retirement age for cars, so we traded it in on a used Volkswagen Rabbit. We were impressed by the used-car salesman's sincerity and helpfulness, and we told him so. He surprised us by saying, "Thank you. The things you admire in my attitude are the areas in which I've been trying to let God take control. I owe it to Him." We can misuse this kind of situation to degrade ourselves: "You sang wonderfully today." "Thanks—I'm a lousy singer, but God made it sound good." Yet, if we keep in mind that good qualities come from our use of God's principles and gifts, we can balance an appreciation for God and a healthy self-concept.

3. The lives of distant saints. By "distant" I mean temporally as well as spatially, and by saints I mean any Christians who are allowing God to work in their lives. Distant saints, therefore, include biblical and church-history figures as well as contemporary Christian writers and missionaries. We can dwell on Sister Teresa's work among lepers in India and thank God for that praiseworthy expression of love. We can thank God for the lofty mind of St. Paul, who filled his letters with spiritual helps for us. (When we think of our own letters, we can more fully appreciate Paul's lofty mind. Suppose Philippians 4 had been written in this manner: "The weather here in Rome is really nice, though I don't get to see much of it. I moved into a new cell yesterday; it has twelve bars across the front and a small cot." A dozen letters in the New Testament like that would get stale pretty quickly.)

4. The lives of local saints. Suppose someone in your church or prayer group has been consistent in providing transportation for the elderly: Thank God for that example of faithfulness. Perhaps someone else, in the middle of a depressing situation, is able to be cheery toward others: Thank God for that example of joy. And as Paul states near the end of the Philippians passage, the ultimate goal of thinking on these things is to put them into practice.

This entire passage, incidentally, resembles Paul's conclusion to his first Thessalonian letter. It contains the well-known, often misunderstood phrase, "Pray unceasingly" (1 Thessalonians 5:17). This verse—like the parable in Luke 11—is used to support persistent prayer in the sense of pestering God daily about our worries and problems. But as we have seen in this chapter, it is neither God's will nor an emotional help for us to pour out the same problems in prayer day after day. In this case, as in many others, a look at the context of the verse is instructive.

> *Always be cheerful. Pray unceasingly. Under all circumstances give thanks, for such is God's will for you in Christ Jesus (1 Thessalonians 5:16–18).*

Both this passage and Philippians 4:4–9 imply that rejoicing and thanksgiving are key elements in ceaseless prayer. People often ask, "What is God's will?" That is a complex question, and in a given situation it is sometimes impossible to determine His complete will. But the last verse above definitely teaches part of God's will in all things: We are to give thanks. When we try to rejoice despite flat tires and to thank God despite medical bills, He will make us "more than conquerors" over worry.

Putting Prayer Into Practice

1. While 1 Thessalonians 5:18 encourages us to be thankful *during* everything, Ephesians 5:20 urges us to be thankful *for* everything. That is sometimes a very different matter. During an illness, for instance, try to see what God might be doing. Does it give you extra time with your family, more time to pray, greater reliance on Him? Think back to the problems you've had this past month and thank God for something about each one.

2. There is value in sharing a burdensome problem. Galatians 6:2 says, "Carry one another's burden and thus fulfill the law of Christ." On the other hand, this must be balanced with Galatians 6:5: "For each person has his own load to

carry." The Greek word translated "load" is the emotional or spiritual equivalent of a small grocery sack, while the word translated "burden" equals a large, heavy trunk. It is good to pray over a problem with someone else if (1) we don't continually take minor problems to people, and (2) we don't take the same major problem to person after person. This would be virtually the same as taking it to God day after day after day. And we must remember our responsibility to others. When someone tells us of a distressing situation, she may not feel comfortable asking us to pray about it. Therefore we should tell her that we would like to pray about it with her.

3. Has God delivered you from a worry in the recent past, or is He in the process of doing so? Although we do not have to ask repeatedly for deliverance, it is highly beneficial, as 1 Thessalonians 5 implies, to rejoice and thank God several times for deliverance from a specific worry.

It's Not Easy

8

MY DAD IS A GRIZZLED FARMER WHO IS MELLOWING WITH AGE and grandchildren. My mom is something like Martha of the New Testament, but busier. Having grown up during the Great Depression, they are both thoroughly imbued with the work ethic. Determine, then, the consequences during my school days of this imaginary conversation:

Dad: Marvin, today I want you to weed the southwest quarter of the garden.

Me: Southwest?

Dad: By the barbecue pit, Marvin!

Me: Oh. Well, I'm sorry, but I just don't feel like it today.

Mom: What's the matter? Are you sick?

Me: No, Mom, nothing like that. It's just that I'm trying to develop a personal relationship with the garden.

Dad: Personal relationship?

Me: Yeah, I don't want my time with the garden to be all planned and lined out, with certain work to be done at certain times. I want to keep my relationship with the garden spontaneous.

Mom: You're going to be spontaneous with a garden?

Me: Yeah, I don't want my work there to be forced; I want to be drawn by the magnetism, the awesomeness of the garden. When I get finished weeding I want an emotional response. I want to feel something. Do you understand?

Dad: That I understand. But if you don't go to the garden you'll *really* feel something. Do *you* understand?

Me: Where's the hoe?

Prayer, like gardening, is hard work. But because it doesn't involve physical labor, many people want to equate an hour of prayer with an hour of bowling: It should be pleasurable and stimulating. Paul did not see prayer in that light, however, as Colossians 4:2 testifies: "Keep persevering in prayer; attend to it diligently with the offering of thanks." This verse follows a passage on being a servant; four verses earlier Paul made this statement:

> *Whatever you do, work heartily as for the Lord and not for men, for you know that from the Lord you will receive the reward of the inheritance. It is Christ the Lord for whom you are working (Colossians 3:23–24).*

Paul's mind does not jump randomly. Apparently the efforts of servants for their masters reminded Paul of the effort involved in regular prayer. But in our century, equating prayer with strenuous work is an unpopular idea.

I do not mean to put down the defenders of spontaneous, unplanned prayer with God. That concept is a natural and even laudatory reaction to the formal, ritualistic prayers of the past. Amid utterances of "O Thou Unknowable, Thou Most Efficacious, Eternal Supreme Sovereign," it was easy to forget that God is our Father, and Christ our Best Friend and Husband (since the church is His bride). The argument for spontaneous prayer insists, "We are to Christ as a wife is to a husband. Does a wife have to make appointments to talk with her husband? Can't she just talk with him whenever she has something to say? What wife would plan an evening discussion with her husband by making a list of conversation topics? Aren't their most precious moments together the spontaneous chats born out of love?"

That's compelling logic and I hesitate to attack it. Undeniably a spontaneous meeting with Christ can be both moving and meaningful. And just as one of the failures of many marriages is the loss of romance, so the failure of many "spiritual marriages" can be traced to a loss of enchantment with Christ. The church at Ephesus worked hard, but Christ sharply (or sadly?) rebuked it, saying, "You have given up your first love" (Revelation 2:4).

Despite all that, there is warrant even from this analogy for setting regular times and places for prayer, making lists of prayer items throughout the day, and planning our times together with God.

Shortly after I became engaged to Audrey, a friend was explaining to me the "ins-and-outs" of wedded life. Since my friend was a veteran of nearly two years of marital happiness, I eagerly listened. "Marv, when I got married, I had dreams of what our conversation would be like," Larry said. "Politics, theology, literature, romance—would you like to hear what we really talk about?"

I nodded in rapt attention as Larry carried on an imaginary conversation between himself and his wife.

Larry: I'm home.

Phyllis: How was your day?

Larry: Fine. How was yours?

Phyllis: Fine. What did we get in the mail?

Larry: A bill from the water company.

Phyllis: That reminds me. The washer broke down today. Can you fix it?

Larry: I'll look at it after supper. What are we having?

Phyllis: Boiled chicken livers.

Larry: I'll look at it now.

My first quarrel with nothing but spontaneity and emotional response in relationships is a pragmatic one: Those qualities don't last. Larry and Phyllis are both articulate college graduates; they assumed that each day they would stimulate one another's thinking. But they don't—not always. And I suspect Larry's account is reasonably close to the norm for most American marriages. (After six years of marriage, I can testify he pictured at least one couple's conversation accurately!)

The point is, in any marriage relationship, *unless we make a deliberate effort to plan them, our conversations with our spouses will tend to become standardized repetitions of external circumstances.* By relying solely on impulse, couples actually move away from what they want to accomplish.

For example, Audrey and I will not ordinarily have a literary conversation. To do so, we have to prepare. We choose a book, read at the same pace, and talk about it every few chapters. It is not natural for me to come home from teaching with a cheery word or a new idea; I must decide to look for something.

Insofar as prayer is a spiritual marriage relationship, it shares the handicaps—and the possibilities—of a physical marriage. In always attempting unpremeditated prayer, we find that the same thoughts come to mind over and over. How many different things can we think of to praise God for "off the cuff"?

It seems clear that a good prayer relationship combines free, unplanned expressions of gratitude with occasional times of organized worship and interaction. Fortunately there are a variety of meaningful ways to organize one's prayer time. First, though, a warning.

Planning prayer is difficult. It is much easier to do what I have so often done: Lie down and assume that some words and phrases will come into my head. Almost all of us tend toward laziness in prayer. Like Paul, we "do not do what we want to do"; like him we can be thankful that "there is . . . now no condemnation to those who are in Christ Jesus" (Romans 8:1). As a fellow struggler, may I make a suggestion? Try marking one or two days on each calendar month as special days for you to visit with God, just as you would mark the calendar if you were invited to someone's home for dinner. Plan during those times to spend one or two hours with God, having pen, paper, notebook, Bible, a quiet location, list of prayer items, perhaps this book or another source of prayer suggestions, and whatever else you might wish to prepare. Just as two business associates can daily meet in the hall for years without really knowing one another, we can spend five minutes a day with God for quite some time and still only appreciate Him on a superficial level.

One valuable tool for worshiping God is a hymnbook. Many hymns disclose aspects of God that we perhaps have not fully appreciated before, such as His permanence—

> Change and decay in all around I see:
> O Thou who changest not, abide with me!

—or His ability to renew us mentally—

> Reclothe us in our rightful mind; . . .
> Drop thy still dews of quietness,
> Till all our strivings cease;
> Take from our souls the strain and stress,
> And let our ordered lives confess
> The beauty of thy peace.

Two other important things to keep near your prayer location are pen and paper, which have various uses. When you finish praying each day, you can list the people or events for which you prayed. If you do this occasionally for several weeks, at least two positive results will occur: First, you will be able to see ways in which God has blessed those people or events; second, when you look back at the problems that distressed you or someone else so terribly three months ago, they often seem relatively less crucial. You will be reminded how transient most of our problems are, particularly when they are contrasted with the permanence of God.

Also, making a list before your prayer time can be helpful. Take a note card to a church service, for instance, and during spare moments write down items from conversations, the program, or the service that merit prayer. Most of us chat with several people after the morning service; if you do, then on returning home, write down something a person said for which you can pray. After praying, ask God to show you how to support that person, by means of a specific action that will affirm your prayer. This might be providing a meal, baby-sitting, making an encouraging phone call, lending a book, working out together, or sharing a verse of Scripture. Sometimes it may be simply telling the person that you prayed for him.

A friend, Daryl, is working full-time and carrying a two-thirds academic load in college. He has a wife and two children. When I talked with Barbie, his wife, she made this perceptive statement: "Marv, a couple of people at church tonight told Daryl they know the pressures he is under, and they are praying for him. That was one of the kindest things they could have done. Daryl sometimes feels as if no one understands how difficult this is for him or why he can't be involved in most church activities at this time." So telling someone you have prayed for him can be a valuable service.

Often it is effective to organize your prayer thoughts around a specific topic. Once a week, for example, I pray exclusively for forgiveness of sins. To keep from being too general, I pray through a list that in medieval times was called "the Seven Deadly Sins": Lust, Pride, Wrath, Gluttony, Greed, Sloth, and Despair. I consider each subject and examine my life to see what specific thoughts or acts I have committed during the week in that category. I ask God's forgiveness for each specific sin and thank Him for specific victories in each category. Incidentally, this kind of prayer is especially effective when spoken aloud; hearing all of one's faults recited orally is an excellent aid to humility.

Another method of organization is to ask God for specific ways to please Him, then to open your mind to His thoughts. I usually hold a pen and paper at this time to write down His responses. Sometimes there may seem to be nothing, and then you can proceed to a different kind of prayer; at other times, however, the Holy Spirit will suggest specific changes in action and attitude.

One more organizational pattern that has been particularly meaningful to me is discursive meditation, a discipline that was highly popular in the sixteenth and seventeenth centuries. To meditate discursively, select an incident from the life of Christ such as a particular parable or miracle. (His birth, crucifixion, resurrection, and ascension are especially effective.) Carefully read the portion of the Gospels where this incident occurs. Make sure all the details are in your mind. Then, laying the Bible aside, try to imagine actually being there at that event. Try to see, hear, and feel what a bystander would have seen, heard, and felt. In your mind, watch the entire action take place. At the end, pretend you have approached Jesus and let your thoughts be known to Him. Express amazement, ask questions, adore Him— whatever response seems appropriate. This does not stimulate everyone's thinking, but many people find discursive meditation a meaningful and moving experience.

The important point is always not which approach you use or even whether you have an approach at all. The key factor is learning not to take prayer casually, but, in Paul's words, to "attend to it diligently."

Putting Prayer Into Practice

1. Small-group prayer times can become mere discussions of external circumstances, just as personal prayer times can. Many prayer groups tend to start by asking, "Does anyone have a prayer request?" or "What is happening in your life that you want prayer for?" While there is occasional need for this, constant petitioning generally crowds out awe, thanksgiving, adoration, and confession. Small-group prayer times can be varied in the same ways as private ones. A significant worship experience in my own prayer group came when after ten minutes of prayer, we felt led to spend the rest of the time simply quoting lines from hymns and Scripture to God.

61

2. I offer a brief explanation of some of "the Seven Deadly Sins," if you wish to consider them. Lust includes all sexual fantasy experience. Despair is a focusing on our problems rather than on God, a lack of confidence in His ability to overcome them. Sloth is not just laziness; it is failure to actively seek out good works to perform and good uses of time. You may feel that with such broad definitions, no one can possibly keep from sinning in some way—and you are right. That is why we have a Savior.

A Glass of Milk, a Chocolate Cake, and Thou

9

WHEN GOD ASKED ADAM IN THE GARDEN OF EDEN, "WHERE ARE you?" He was not requesting information. God was giving Adam a chance to confess his sin, leading him toward an understanding of the error.

I often think that the same sort of dialogue would help us to understand our own regular failures in prayer and righteous living. Consider what would happen if Jeff Pixler, typical Christian, were interrupted tonight during his nightly prayer. Jeff is lying in his bed, fluffy pillow over his eyes and forehead, listening to his wife Marjorie's light snoring. He exhales deeply and begins silently to pray.

"Dear God, Marjorie doesn't know about it yet, but you already know about that cake tonight. How could I eat half a chocolate cake in ten minutes? Anyway, since it was obviously gluttony on my part, please forgive me and . . ."

"Jeff."

Startled, our subject shakes off the pillow and opens his eyes, but the room is empty. He sees Marjorie asleep under the checkered quilt. Then, remembering the story of Samuel, Jeff responds: "Speak, Lord, your servant hears."

"Jeff, did you know ahead of time that your wife had a teachers' meeting tonight and would be gone?"

"Uh-huh."

"Did you know the chocolate cake was in the oven?"

"Uh-huh."

"Have you ever in your entire life been satisfied with just one piece of chocolate cake?"

"Huh-uh." Jeff pulls the quilt up a bit and mulls the situation over. "I guess my prayer is about six hours late," he finally admits.

It is not surprising Jeff prayed six hours too late. Advance prayer against temptation is rare. Yet the need for it is demonstrated in one of the New Testament's most familiar stories.

> *They came to a place called Gethsemane, and He told His disciples, "Be seated here while I pray." But He took along with Him Peter, James and John, and as He began to feel deeply alarmed and distressed, He said to them, "My soul is mortally grieved; stay here and watch." Going a little farther, He fell on the ground and prayed that, if possible, the impending hour might pass from Him. He said, "Abba, Father, all things are possible with Thee. Remove this cup from Me. Not, however, what I will but what Thou wilt."*
>
> *He came and found them asleep, and said to Peter, "Simon, are you sleeping? Were you not able to watch for one hour? All of you watch and pray, so that you may not enter into temptation. The spirit is willing enough, but the flesh is weak."*
>
> *He left again and prayed, uttering the same words. Then He returned to find them asleep once more; for their eyes were heavy. And they did not know what excuse to give Him. He then came for the third time and said to them "Sleeping and resting still? It is enough; the hour has come" (Mark 14:32–41).*

Just before this event, Peter, James, and John had asserted their faithfulness to Christ, declaring that they would never turn away from Him or deny Him. (Many people think only Peter made that statement, but verse 31 corrects that misconception.) Christ takes these three aside, as the ones to whom He is closest, and charges them to "watch" while He prays. Watch what—Him? Each other?

One New Testament meaning of "watch" is to watch in

order to guard. Jesus appears to be putting these disciples on sentry duty, and so He is, though not against the Roman soldiers. They are to guard against the night's coming temptations.

A chief sign of maturity in the Christian life is an effort to move from praying after temptation to praying before it. Praying before temptation is an indication of increasing love for God, and love, of course, is the foremost commandment. Besides being described as a Judge, Benefactor, and Father, God is also referred to in the Bible as our Husband. This analogy illustrates why deep love prays in advance.

The finest book of our time on how husbands can please their wives is probably H. Page Williams's *Do Yourself a Favor: Love your Wife.*[1] Williams observes that many husbands buy gifts for their wives on special occasions without determining what the wife's favorite color or scent is. A truly loving husband, Williams notes, will find out in advance what does or does not thrill his wife, so he can make himself more pleasing to her.

Christians often overlook the serious implications of this for spiritual discipline. A temptation is, in effect, a special occasion when we are either going to please God or disappoint Him. For a special occasion, a husband has two choices: He can wait until the moment comes to choose a gift and hope that a spur-of-the-moment decision will please his wife, or he can ask her in advance for information if he wants to be sure of doing the right thing. Similarly, we may be aware of potential temptations well in advance. We can hope that at the moment of decision we will automatically choose correctly, or we can talk the situation over with God ahead of time, asking Him to remind us of what He wants when the moment comes.

I am aware, of course, that many temptations come on suddenly. At such times we have no recourse but to go to

---

[1](South Plainfield, N.J.: Bridge Publishing Co., 1979).

God in an instant. But sometimes, as with Jeff and his chocolate cake, we know hours beforehand when we will face a difficult decision. We know that sometime next week at work Bill will tell another dirty joke, and we'll have to decide whether to ignore it, walk away, or express disapproval. We know that if we give a good speech, we'll be tempted to feel proud. If we come home from work with a bad headache, we know we'll tend to be grouchier than usual with our families.

Certain situations scream out for prayer. On shopping trips, we already know that stores will offer attractive, inviting merchandise in abundance, with appealing promotions. We know we will find something we want but don't need. We can ask God in advance to control our thoughts while we are in the store. It may be that, having prayed, we will still buy the same items; but we will have done it "in the name of the Lord Jesus." This does not mean we have to pray about every coming decision—rather, only those where one choice might be self-centered. We don't need to pray tonight about what color slacks or skirt we will wear tomorrow; neither decision will be sinful.

If we do not pray about our temptations, we will usually give in to them. Satan is simply too much stronger than we are. I have to pray before a major trip to keep from breaking the law, because out on the road I can find numerous justifications for going sixty miles per hour. (I'm tired, it's going to rain, we might be late.)

Audrey and I decided to buy a television set. It seemed a reasonable thing to do, because with Audrey working, TV would entertain Rocky for ten hours a week while I was writing. We prayed about it and both felt positively that it was within God's permissive will for us to buy a used black-and-white portable set. Accordingly we bought one for $30.

But while driving home, we saw a sidewalk sale at another store. Noticing several TVs, we decided to take a look at them, not intending to buy but to congratulate ourselves on how much money we had saved. One of the sets was a beautiful, full-size color TV with touch-tuning, remote control, and a sharp picture for only $298.

"Isn't that a super price!" Audrey exclaimed.

"Yes, it is," I said, thinking rapidly. In *One Woman's Liberation*, Shirley Boone claims jokingly that among her husband Pat's spiritual gifts is the "gift of rationalization." Mine was now coming forward. "Sweetheart, you know how lovely and green the English countryside is in those BBC Shakespeare plays?"

"Yes," Audrey agreed. "You wouldn't be happy seeing those in black-and-white, would you?"

As we discussed the exciting possibility of watching "Star Trek" and "Sha-Na-Na" (our two favorite shows) in color, the idea of "a TV for Rocky" was rapidly replaced by "a TV for us." A full-size color TV now sits comfortably in the middle of our living room.

Whether TV is good or evil is not the point. The point is that for us, this purchase was a sin. We did not buy the second set after seeking God's approval, out of wanting to please Him, but we bought it to satisfy our selfishness.

Our sin could easily have been avoided with prayer. Suppose we had retired to the car upon first desiring that TV set. Even while asking God for wisdom regarding whether to make the purchase, we would have guiltily realized that in no way could buying a TV that expensive be, for us, a fulfillment of Colossians 3:17: "Whatever you do by word or deed, do it all in the name of the Lord Jesus."

In a more positive example of anticipatory prayer, Audrey and I recently invited Sandy, a young nurse, to our home for lunch. We decided that rather than praying before the meal, the three of us would pray about our time together before Sandy left. Before we began to pray, Sandy remarked that she was being shifted to a different floor of the hospital that evening. She was somewhat irritated and afraid she would have an angry attitude toward her supervisor. Sandy asked

Audrey and me to pray that she would humbly submit to her supervisor in attitude as well as in action. The three of us shared a meaningful time of asking for God's protection.

The following Sunday, Sandy glowingly told Audrey that she had entered the hospital ready to offer her services up to God that evening. Despite her less pleasant circumstances, Sandy was able to remember that she was working primarily to please God. Would she have had this attitude without prayer? I doubt it. God does not force new personalities on us; He changes us when we ask for it.

A woman in our church once said that many of our attitudes as Christians boil down to a simple question: "Do I really trust God?" It's a powerful question, and alongside it I would place "Do I really love God?" If we do, we will certainly spend part of our prayer time looking for upcoming temptations, anxious to avoid everything that will not glorify God.

Putting Prayer Into Practice

1. Think of occasions in the past in which you have sinned. Will you be faced with a similar situation during the next day or two? Pray about it.

2. One situation is such a common and serious source of temptation that I mention it separately. Will you be spending a great deal of time privately with a member of the opposite sex? Counseling and conferences can cause great difficulty, but if prayed about, they can be times of triumph and satisfaction. Two years ago I had to work closely with a student teacher who was intelligent, enthusiastic, devout, and attractive. For eight weeks I prayed regularly that during each daily meeting God would cause me to see her not as a source of sensual pleasure, but as a complete person to guide toward professional maturity. Today the correspondence Audrey and I have with her and her husband is a great joy and edification to us. If you will be encountering a similar situation, pray about it; God can turn frustration into contentment.

A Different Kind of Spiritual Gift   10

IT IS 12:03 P.M. ON A PLEASANT SPRING SUNDAY. SERVICE HAS ended a few minutes late at Elm Street Chapel. Yet no one feels pressured to rush home and rescue a scorching roast; the crockpots and Kentucky Fried Chickens are doing their prescribed tasks. Ah, the twentieth century!

In the foyer Gene Hirt has been chatting with Scott Berry. "Say, Scott, I thanked God for you yesterday."

"You did? How come?" Scott asks, surprised.

"I was thinking about how kind you and your wife are to Mrs. Bennett. She told me how you-all not only take her to church every Sunday, but on the way home you stop at the grocery store so she can pick up some things. You've been a real example to me, and I thanked God for letting me get to know you."

"Thanks, Gene, I really appreciate that."

Can you imagine this conversation taking place in your church? Or will the talk more likely center on the weather and the Cardinals-Giants game?

Most of us as Christians claim to follow the teaching and example of the New Testament as much as possible. Yet it is curious that the most common type of prayer in the New Testament is one of the rarest today. That prayer is not for healing, for evangelism, or for forgiveness, but thankfulness for other people.

Surprised? A quick trip through Paul's epistles will back up that statement. Consider Romans 1:8: "To begin with, I certainly thank my God for all of you through Jesus Christ, because your faith is being mentioned all over the world."

And 1 Corinthians 1:4—5: "Always I thank my God for you, for the divine grace that has through Christ Jesus been granted you; for in Him you have in every respect been enriched with full power of expression and full knowledge."

And 1 Thessalonians 1:3—4: "We are always bound to give God thanks for you, brothers, as is befitting, because your faith is growing so splendidly and the love of each of you for one another is increasing, so that we ourselves mention you with pride among the churches of God for your fortitude and faith amid all the persecutions and distresses which you endure."

And Ephesians 1:15—16 and Colossians 1:3—5 and 2 Timothy 1:3—5 and . . .

In recent years there has been a strong interest in spiritual gifts in the church. Yet too few of us seem to realize that one certain gift is possessed by the entire Christian community. In a very real sense, we are God's spiritual gifts to each other.

There are three steps involved in thanking God for others. The first is to do it often. I think one of the most astounding verses in the New Testament is Philippians 1:3, where Paul says, "Every time I think of you I thank my God." (Have you ever noticed how often Paul uses words like "ceaselessly" and "continually" regarding his prayer life? When I consider my own, I find it a bit humiliating.) Prayer should be the primary time each day when our minds move off ourselves and onto others. Yet I fear the amount of time we spend praying about ourselves and about others rarely balances. Thanking God for others, helps to restore this balance.

But simply thanking God for each person's existence can

easily become ritualized: "Thank You for Jane and Arnie and Steve and Frieda and . . ." Therefore the second step in this kind of prayer is to thank God for something specific in a person's life. Notice how Paul does this even when he's writing to an entire congregation rather than an individual. In the case of the Romans, he thanks God for their faith; the Corinthians, for their power of expression and knowledge; the Thessalonians, for their faith and mutual love.

The third step is difficult, yet quite important. We need to tell others after we have thanked God for them. It doesn't have to be in person; Paul communicates his message through a letter. But it is valuable, both for us and for the other person, to let the prayer of thanks be known.

To illustrate: Audrey and I invited Dillard and Bev to supper. Audrey prepared her famous taco pizza, and as usual, each biteful was delightful. I faced three choices. First, I could stuff myself with pizza and not bother to thank Audrey at all. Fortunately I know my husbandly role better than that.

Second, I could wait until Dillard and Bev left before saying, "Audrey, that supper was magnificent! You are the Chris Evert Lloyd of pizza." That's better, but it still doesn't convey the full sense of my appreciation.

Third, I could take a few bites of taco pizza to verify its greatness and thank Audrey for it in our guests' presence. That's what I'd typically do, and, in essence, that's what we're doing when we tell someone we've thanked God for her. We're thanking her before God, in His presence.

Thanking God for what someone else has done is helpful in several ways. It focuses some of our prayer thoughts on others. It reminds them that their good deeds belong to God. It encourages them to continue doing good. And it builds up unity within the body of Christ.

The last point is worth considering further. Many churches today severely lack fellowship in the true sense. We try to make up for it with potluck dinners and coffee hours, but too often we don't have the Christ-centered, intertwined thoughts and lives of the early church. The title of a splendid book, *Crowded Pews and Lonely People,* says it all.[1] Thanking God for another person's action or attitude helps us to view him or her as a Christian servant instead of merely as a dentist or an accountant. The expression of thanks brings a closeness that Christians too seldom experience.

"But I can't do that! I can't just go up to somebody at church and tell him I thanked God for him this week. I'd feel uncomfortable." So do I. But Christ didn't say, "Take up your cross if you feel comfortable with it and follow Me."

If you are concerned about making the other person feel uncomfortable, don't be. Your experience will very likely resemble my first time.

Me: (slightly embarrassed) Ellen, thank you for having Audrey and me over to sing hymns Friday night.

Ellen: Oh, we enjoyed it.

Me: Audrey told me yesterday that you invite people over to your house once a month to do that.

Ellen: Well, since I have a piano, I consider it sort of a praise ministry.

Me: When I was praying last night, I thought about that and thanked God for creating you and the way you invite people over like that.

Ellen: What a nice thing! (seriously) You know, I think that's the first time in my whole life I ever heard of anyone thanking God for me. People always thank me, but don't thank God for me. That makes me feel like someone special to Him. Thank you.

Putting Prayer Into Practice

1. Sometime in a prayer group, spend the main portion of the prayer time thanking God for others. They can be either members of the group or mutual acquaintances. Remember to look for specific attitudes and actions that express Chris-

[1]M. L. Jacobsen (Wheaton, Ill.: Tyndale, 1972).

tianity—examples of hospitality, charity, service, humility, wisdom, and so on. If the person for whom you thanked God is not in the group, contact her during the week.

2. There may be people in the church whom you do not care for. Ask God to point out to you ways in which they honor Him. You'll find, I believe, that expressing gratitude to God for those people will greatly increase your charitable feelings toward them.

Are Two Heads Better Than One? 11

AUDREY, ROCKY, AND I WERE IN JOHNNY AND DORA'S HOME. We were celebrating the completion of the first half of this book with homemade strawberry shakes. Their six-month-old baby was contentedly gnawing my index finger when Johnny asked a question.

"Marv, I can understand why it's not necessary to ask God for a particular object over and over again. But is that the same as asking someone else to pray about it?"

Dora also had a question. "And what about the verse 'if two of you are agreed'? Does that mean the prayers of two people work better than the prayers of one person?"

Johnny and Dora's questions are insightful. If two people praying is better than one, wouldn't three be even better? And ten better yet? And a thousand? On the other hand, if the prayer of two people is not better than the prayer of one, then what's the use of ever asking someone else to pray for me? Why can't I just do all my praying alone?

I think Dora's question about two being better than one would be answered if we could have heard Jesus say those words. (In English.) Matthew 18:19–20 says, "Once more I assure you that if two of you are agreed on earth about anything for which you pray, it will be done for you by My heavenly Father. For where two or three have gathered in My name, I am there with them." The accented word is not "two," but "agreed."

Jesus' point is not that prayers are made more effective by adding another person. He is indicating that when two people—or more, as implied in verse 20—gather in His name to pray, they must be agreed for their prayers to be effective.

Because Jesus' words are stated in a context of church structure, I will illustrate with a church example. I once attended a congregation in which the members of the church board expressed something less than *agape* love. The board meetings were always opened with a sanctimonious prayer of the type I mentioned in chapter 3—a "prayer of introduction." The closing "Amen" of that prayer was their signal to verbally attack one another. I would guess that those church board meetings caused more headaches and ulcers than could ever be caused at a PTA or Elks Club meeting. Each man went home fuming at the "stubborn pigheadedness" of the other members.

The church failed to grow, spiritually or any other way. Yet the prayers offered at the board meetings seemed as full of plans and possibilities as those in any church. The obvious reason why the prayers of this church were not answered is that the board members did not agree.

Another argument against the idea that the prayers of two people are more powerful is that it makes our effort in prayer more important than God's. We would be asserting that God is limited by our ability to gather people together, that our "weakness" (a one-person prayer) would cause Him to be weak. On the contrary, God asserts in 2 Corinthians 12:9, "My strength comes to perfection where there is weakness."

Johnny's question is more complex than Dora's. It gets to the heart of what prayer is expected to do. His is another "What's the use?" question: What's the use of praying for another person?

I wrote earlier that we do not just pray for material things in order to receive them, but also to honor God. Yet, when we pray for a person instead of a thing, another reason enters in: *Praying for another person causes us to become less self-centered and makes it much easier for us to love and identify with that person,* whether an enemy or a friend.

Evidence for this in regard to enemies comes from Christ's Sermon on the Mount. The primary point of that lecture is the extension from action (teaching of the law) to attitude (teaching of Christ). Under Christ's dominion, the adultery prohibition is expanded to include lust, and the murder prohibition is enlarged to include wrath. Near the end of Matthew 5, love is extended to include even enemies, and Christ suggests a way of implementing that love: "Pray for your persecutors" (v. 44). Loving our enemies is such an unnatural act that we cannot do it on our own. Of course, we can ignore our enemies, we can forget what they've done, we can make an effort (for business or neighborhood reasons) to get along; but we cannot naturally love those who antagonize us.

In our prayer group we had discussed the importance of showing love to enemies as well as friends, and Dora prayed that God would give her an opportunity to do that. The opportunity knocked quickly.

Each morning at about seven o'clock Johnny says good-by to Dora by hitting the car horn once. One Tuesday morning after Johnny had been gone several minutes, the next-door neighbor, whom Dora didn't really know, knocked on her door.

"Hello," the neighbor said. "I'd like you to ask your husband to quit honking the horn in the morning. It bothers me."

He strode away, and Dora shut her door angrily. *The nerve of that guy!* she thought. *A little tap on the horn couldn't bother him at all! Why does he have to make such a big deal out of it?*

As Dora continued fuming through her day, she suddenly realized that this was exactly what she had asked for—an opportunity to love an enemy and pray for a "persecutor."

She prayed for her neighbor and for what would please God and felt led to bake an apple pie. Dora tells the rest of the story in her own words.

"It was the most perfect pie I had ever baked—even the little scallops around the edges turned out right! My neighbors weren't home when the pie was done, so I left it on the table to cool. You know, every time I saw that pie the rest of the day I just felt so happy, bubbling over with joy, like I'd really been able to make God happy in a small way."

As a postscript to that incident, the neighbors proved to be quite friendly, and they were amazed at receiving the pie. With such results available through prayer for enemies, the result of prayer for friends is bound to be astounding—and it is.

Suppose that Greg Bolick is unemployed and asks his friend Blake Crowley to pray for him. Blake, who works for the U.S. Postal Service, has good health and a happy family and has been blissfully unaware of the struggles of some people in his congregation. Taking this prayer responsibility seriously, he is forced to recognize Greg's feelings. When Blake prays that evening, he thinks about the financial pressures on the Bolick family, who bought a house just two years ago. He thinks about Greg's humiliation in being laid off and not working for his family, the idle hours around the house wondering at his age what kind of position he can find. Because Blake is praying about Greg's difficulties, taking them as seriously as he does his own, he is able to fulfill Romans 12:15: "Share the joy of those who are happy and the grief of those who grieve."

At this point, having fully empathized with Greg, Blake is able to do what Greg may find difficult to do. Blake can ask God for spiritual guidance and thank Him for the positive aspects of the situation. He may see, for instance, that unemployment is causing Greg to depend more on God than on personal earning power. Blake may thank God that Greg has extra time to help his wife around the house and to grow spiritually through prayer and Christian reading.

Finally, Blake will pray about ways to serve and to encourage Greg during this struggle. This may include praying together, telling Greg what he feels Greg can be thankful for, sympathizing with him, challenging him to learn something new—cooking? cabinet-making?—or giving financial help. Whether or not Greg agrees with these suggestions, he will be glad that Blake is at least taking the job loss seriously. There will be a closeness between the two of them that was absent in their earlier, superficial relationship.

A request for prayer is an invitation to look beyond the external qualities of occupation, family, and recreation to a person's very thoughts and feelings. Christians too often use the phrase "I'll pray about it" flippantly. If we actually do agree to make another person's request our own, we should attempt to agree fully, in the sense of Matthew 18:19. We should pray to God as fervently as if the problem were our own.

We all have limitations of time and energy. Therefore, if our church or prayer group is in the habit of tossing out a dozen or more prayer requests at a time, we should not add all of them to our personal prayer lists. If we do, we will almost certainly fail to take the request as seriously as the person making it does. In other words, we will not be in complete effective agreement with her prayer.

Suppose you are asked by fifteen different people to help them build tool sheds next week. You have two choices. First, you could attempt to help everyone; you could stir the paint at Nacrellis', drill some holes at Mulfords', caulk the windows at Conklins', and do ten-minute jobs at a dozen other houses. You hardly expect to gain a sense of fellowship with the Nacrellis from stirring their paint.

Or you could spend an entire afternoon building a shed with the Veaches. Either way you've done the same amount of work; but when you shake hands with Mr. and Mrs. Veach at dinnertime and look back at the structure, something has changed. You know what the Veaches have gone through, and they're aware that you know. You've struggled together and have built not only a tool shed, but a relationship. Half of praying for another person is "it will be done"; the other half is "I am there with them."

Putting Prayer Into Practice

1. The early church took Christ's command about praying for persecutors seriously. Stephen, the first martyr, called out, "Lord, do not hold this sin against them," as he was being stoned. While we may not now have persecution in the physical sense, sometimes we undergo (or think we do) emotional and mental harassment. Who is your "enemy"—a boss, neighbor, even a spouse? Pray for that person, forgiving him or her, asking God to forgive, and asking God if you should do a particular act of love for him or her. That person may reject it; but if the act of love is done for God, that will not matter as much.

2. Set aside a day each week during which you will pray for someone other than yourself. Be alert for prayer opportunities; each week concentrate on a different person or situation. Go through the three steps: Empathize with that person's response to his or her circumstances; thank God for His control and any positive benefits in the situation; and see if you can support or encourage that person somehow. If you begin doing this and encourage others to do so, fellowship in your church will become more than a dinner or coffee hour.

Praying for Grain   12

GENERALLY SPEAKING, WORLDLY HUMANS UNDERSTAND HOW to deal with people better than Christians do. That's a rash statement and one that I would hate to have to defend. Fortunately, I don't have to, because I didn't make it; Jesus did: "The sons of this world are more astute than the sons of light in their own generation" (Luke 16:8). No matter how one interprets the parable of the dishonest manager (vv. 1–12), the import of that verse is the same. Although Christians ordinarily have loftier goals than non-Christians, we sometimes do not display the Lord's wisdom in reaching for those goals.

During my teenage years on the family farm, we did not have a corn picker, so when harvest time came we always hired it done. Suppose that one year when the corn needs picking our usual helper becomes sick and cannot take care of it. Dad and I discuss the situation.

Dad: Marvin, I want you to put an ad in the newspaper for someone who has a corn picker to come pick our corn.

Me: I have a better idea.

Dad: What's that?

Me: Let's put an ad in the newspaper to the corn, saying that it needs to be harvested.

Dad: What are you talking about? The corn can't read.

Me: But if we put the ad in day after day after day, I'll bet the corn will get picked. I knew one farmer in Madison County who faithfully put in an ad to the corn for seventeen days, and sure enough, his corn was harvested.

Dad: Sure—after some farmer noticed the ad and sent a corn picker through the field.

The illustration is absurd, yet the kind of prayer it ridicules is one of the most common prayers among evangelical Christians. How many times have you heard prayer requests like these?

• "I'd like you-all to pray that my sister, who's not a Christian, will become one."

• "Let's pray that during the Leighton Ford Crusade this week many people will realize their need for Christ."

• "I'm the only Christian on my job, so pray that God will cause someone else to become one."

Most people who pray this way do so out of sincere trust in God. Yet I believe common sense and Scripture teach us a more effective way to pray evangelistically. Consider, for example, Christ's words regarding the multitude's salvation in Matthew 9:37–38: "Then He said to His disciples, 'The harvest is indeed abundant but the workers are few. Therefore pray the Lord of the harvest that He may send out workers into His harvest.'"

Christ specifically teaches the disciples to pray for workers, for harvesters. Indeed, this is the pattern of the entire New Testament. Christ draws a distinction between His followers and the lost in John 17:9 when He says, "I pray for them. *I do not pray for the world* but for those whom Thou hast granted Me, for they belong to Thee" (emphasis mine). In verse 20 of that chapter Christ extends His prayers to all believers, including us: "I am not praying only for them, but also for those who will believe in Me through their message."

The apostle Paul similarly implies that our evangelistic prayers should be given for other Christians rather than for the lost. For example, he asks the Ephesian Christians to pray "for all the saints; also for me, that, when I open my lips, . . . I may announce fearlessly the secret of the good news" (Ephesians 6:18—19). Colossians 4:2—4—a passage we examined earlier—also implies that our primary evangelistic prayers should be for Christian workers and not for the lost. In it Paul requests the Christians at Colossae to "keep persevering in prayer; . . . praying for us also, that God may open for us a door to tell the message of the secret of Christ. . . ." I find no place where Paul asks Christians to pray that unbelievers will be receptive to his message.

Actually we shouldn't even need such explicit references in Scripture to recognize where our prayer efforts should be directed. The image of the field in Matthew 9 should make our duties clear. We know that the "Lord of the harvest" (God) wants the grain harvested; even if the Gospels did not yield that impression, nothing could be plainer than 2 Peter 3:9: "The Lord is . . . unwilling that any should perish, but that all should come to repentance."

To pray, therefore, that God will try to save a certain friend or relative almost implies that we don't believe He has been trying. If we give God a "push" in prayer, we think, then He will take that person's salvation seriously. Yet God already cares for each person He has created far more than we ever could. A good illustration of this truth occurs in *The Magician's Nephew*, book 6 of C. S. Lewis's *Chronicles of Narnia*. Young Digory Kirke has entered the magic land of Narnia hoping to find a cure for his mother. ("Kirk," by the way, is the Scottish word for "church.") When Aslan the Lion, who represents Christ, bends down toward Digory, the boy is surprised to see that "great shining tears stood in the lion's eyes. They were such big, bright tears compared with Digory's own that for a moment he felt as if the Lion must really be sorrier about his Mother than he was himself."[1]

[1](New York: Macmillan, 1970), ch. 12.

Some people, on the other hand, claim that we should pray for the lost to realize their lost condition. But how do they recognize their lost condition? Either through God's influence (and God is already doing His part) or through being told by a Christian. If that is the case, it would seem more beneficial to pray for the Christian than for the non-Christian, for we can then share our prayers with that Christian to encourage him or her. In addition, the Holy Spirit has greater control of the life of the Christian, and therefore the Christian is more likely to be influenced by our prayers than is the non-Christian.

So what is our responsibility in evangelistic prayers? We are to pray for ourselves and others that as Christian witnesses we will sensitively, courageously, and accurately declare the message of Christ. Christ's analogies make this apparent.

Jesus compares the lost to, among other things, grain, poor soil, shepherdless sheep, weeds, and the ill. All these metaphors imply that our primary task is to influence, not the lost themselves, but those who can help the lost. If several sheep have escaped from a pasture (the parable of the lost sheep), we don't implore them to return; we tell the shepherd and offer our services in helping to bring them back. If we are hired hands working for a farmer (the parable of the sower), we do not ask him to help the soil realize it's rocky; we ask him for digging tools to clear the rocks away so his seed can enter the ground more easily.

What does this mean for our prayer life? Our evangelistic prayers should concentrate on harvesters rather than grain. Of the two hundred or more non-Christians we personally contact each month, probably very few are ready at this time to accept Christ. If we direct our prayers toward our office partners, for instance, we will likely focus much of our evangelistic efforts on them. Yet they may not be mentally and emotionally ready to accept Christ for eight years yet, and even then it might not be through our influence. Meanwhile, the custodian at work may be going through real spiritual trauma and be eager to hear of Christ; yet we ignore him in an effort to reach the office partner.

The better way is to pray for God's wisdom for ourselves. We should ask the Holy Spirit to help us see which people are ready, which ones He is preparing. Then, filled with heavenly courage and understanding, we should see which people around us are interested in a spiritual conversation.

Our prayer with another person should be conducted in the same way. Why should we ask a prayer partner to pray for a sister's salvation when she has indicated complete disinterest in Christ for the past decade? While God works miracles, He does not force Himself on people. But if that sister responds with interest to learning about Christ, we might very well wish someone to pray with us for wisdom in answering her questions or for patience with her slow response.

In this matter, as in so many others, our natural tendency is to pray for external changes ("Sell my house, heal my spouse") when what God wants is internal change ("Give me patience, give me love"). To ask God to save someone we love is, on the human level, about as high as one can reach. But to ask God to let us see with His eyes, to make us want to tell His grace even to people we don't care for, is sublime.

Putting Prayer Into Practice

1. Every month spend part of your prayer time praying that God will make you sensitive to people's feelings concerning Christianity. Ask Him for courage to start conversations on the subject and wisdom to see if the other person is interested. If you're not sure what to say, a good book on the subject—both spiritually discerning and delightful to read—is *Out of the Salt Shaker* by Rebecca Manley Pippert (Downers Grove, Ill.: InterVarsity Press, 1979).

2. Perhaps you want to be sure that God is working in a person's life before sharing Christ with her. I think it is perfectly appropriate to ask God for a specific conversational

sign. For example, you might ask God to have the person say, "You look like you have something on your mind." Or if you plan to say, "What do you usually do on Sundays?" you might ask God to have her respond, "Well, I've been looking for something different." If a sign isn't given, that does not remove your responsibility to evangelize. But when God has prepared a receptive listener and gives you a specific answer, you will find yourself much calmer and bolder about presenting Christ, knowing that He is guiding you. At least it works that way for me.

To Boldly Kneel   13

"SPACE . . . THE FINAL FRONTIER. THESE ARE THE VOYAGES OF the Starship *Enterprise*. Its five-year mission . . . to explore strange new worlds . . . to seek out new life and new civilizations . . . to boldly go where no man has gone before."

Audrey and I were given a small black-and-white portable TV for our marriage (a predecessor of our recent purchase), but we usually watched it only a half-hour each day . . . until Saturday night. At 10:15 P.M. Saturday, "Star Trek" came on; and whenever we heard those familiar opening words, Audrey and I were ready to seek out new life ourselves. The range of exciting possibilities exhilarated us.

In the past two decades, prayer for evangelicals has become a sort of spiritual "Star Trek." For several centuries after the life of Christ, God had remained to most minds a vast, awesome, unapproachable Power. This was, as a matter of fact, the reason the Catholic church began praying through saints. In medieval European life, a commoner could hardly expect to go straight to the king for whatever was needed. Similarly the ordinary peasant could not imagine himself capable of addressing the "King of Kings and Lord of Lords" directly. Therefore he worshiped through a priest and prayed through a saint.

Although the Reformation forged a breakthrough in eliminating corruption, the concept of God remained the same. People began to pray directly to Him, but it was generally with a sense of amazement that He was listening. And so it continued through recent centuries: Christ was loved and adored ("Fairest Lord Jesus"); God was feared and exalted ("A Mighty Fortress").

During the past quarter-century, however, social patterns have changed. Family life was once a hierarchy with the husband as captain, the wife as first mate, and the children as deck hands. Mutinies were rare. Now most marriages are more analogous to small corporations, the husband and wife being business partners, the children junior executives. In addition, fear in families and societies has been greatly reduced. Television shows about the past, such as "Little House on the Prairie" and "The Waltons," downplay this aspect of family life. But in those days, when children did wrong, they trembled: Punishment would be swift, sure, and terrible. On a societal level, theft of a loaf of bread was punishable in Shakespeare's England by loss of a hand. Today judges give relatively mild sentences for minor offenses.

Typically, some of these changes have been beneficial and some detrimental. Either way they have altered our conception of God. Today people are more familiar with Him. In prayer, His most common title now is "Father" rather than "Lord." More people address God with informal "You" rather than the more formal "Thou." (Ironically, "thee" and "thou" were informal words in the time of King James.)

Having been so recently delivered from formal, liturgical speech in talking with God, it is natural for us to feel that we are exploring strange new worlds, that we are going "to boldly kneel where no man has knelt before." On the other hand, our relationship with God should not become too free; He is not our "pal in the sky" or—I shudder when I hear the phrase—"the Man Upstairs." The same chapter in the Bible that gives us permission to approach the throne of grace boldly also warns, "It is dreadful to fall into the hands of the living God" (Hebrews 10:31).

To avoid the twin errors of overfamiliarity and excessive formality, I try to keep in mind the variety of relationships I have with God. The following paragraph offers several metaphors used in Matthew's Gospel to explain in part who God is. This may not seem directly related to prayer—yet our understanding of who God is decidedly affects our conversations with Him. I talk in a different manner and about different subjects with my wife than I do with my son, my students, my principal, or my parents.

God is presented in the Gospel of Matthew in at least eight different images. He is the Supreme Master (6:24), the Father who gives good gifts to His children (7:11), the Lord of the Harvest (9:38), the Potential Destroyer (10:28), the Granter of Requests (18:19), the Creator (19:4), the Estate Owner (20:1), and the King (22:2). Obviously this list could be much longer.

I offer this because it is easy to continually look at God only one way during our prayer times. If we perpetually see Him as the Granter of Requests, we lose sight of His regal qualities. If we always celebrate Him as the Creator, we may become overattached to this world, forgetting that He is also the Destroyer. Most of us, I fear, prefer to view God as the kindly Father who wants to keep us from all discomfort.

Recently I have come to place increasing emphasis on the point at hand, due to my praying with several people more than once. It is thought-provoking how limited our vision can be concerning God. Some people view God solely as the Great Physician. Whenever they make a prayer request at church, it is always for healing—an uncle with a cold, a cousin with the flu. Others see God only as the Best Friend (which He is) and spend virtually all of their prayer time telling God what events are taking place and how they feel.

This makes praying with another person or in a group

quite valuable. We often are shown a different side of God in observing someone else's relationship with Him. I myself tend to see God more often as the Just and Omniscient Judge than in any other way. Praying with a person who is most aware of God's forgiving aspect comforts me and conversely alerts my partner to the seriousness of sin.

We can never comprehend God's totality in this life. All of us see Him indistinctly. But the more we learn of Him, the more we will be filled with awe. Someday perhaps we can reach the transcending wonder Paul felt:

> *O the depth of the wealth, the wisdom, and the knowledge of God! How inscrutable are His judgments and how untraceable His footsteps! For who has understood the Lord's mind, or who has become His counselor? Or who has given anything to Him that it might be repaid him? For from Him, and through Him and to Him are all things. To Him be glory forever! Amen (Romans 11:33–36).*

Putting Prayer Into Practice

Addressing God in a different way not only offers a fresh approach to prayer, but also yields new subject matter. It reveals new attributes to thank God for and appreciate about Him. Once every two or three weeks, start your prayer with another word for God besides "Father" or whatever form of address you normally use. If you think of Him as the Estate Owner, you will thank Him for preparing heaven and sharing it with you. If you think of Him as the Supreme Master, you will thank Him for the way He keeps money, possessions, and friends from being totally satisfying. There is no higher purpose in prayer than getting to know God better.

Prayer and Pizza   14

"MARK, AUDREY AND I WANT TO KNOW IF YOU AND FRANCES would like to come pray with us tomorrow night."

"Sure, Marv. What are we going to play?"

"No, not play. *Pray.*"

"Pray? You mean like in church?"

"Yeah, we want you to come pray with us. Then we'll have something to eat and talk for a while."

"Okay, we'll be there."

Many changes have occurred since the first two centuries of the church. We don't kiss each other at services; we don't dunk people three times (once for each Person of the Trinity) at baptism; we don't celebrate Communion as part of a "love feast." Not all of the changes are detrimental; few of us would wish to continue the early church custom of baptizing people naked!

Perhaps the most regrettable change, however, has been the loss of prayer meetings in homes. The Book of Acts presents a picture of constant prayer meetings: Formal, informal, in public places, in homes, on a riverbank, by the seashore. After Peter and John, arrested for teaching about Jesus, were released by the Sanhedrin, "they went to their own companions and related to them everything that the chief priests and elders had said. Then those who heard it unitedly raised their voices to God. . . . And when they had prayed, their meeting place shook and they were all filled with the Holy Spirit" (Acts 4:23–24, 31).

Sometime later, when Peter was released from prison on a different occasion, he knew where to find a group of Christians: "When he got his bearings he went to the home of Mary, the mother of John, surnamed Mark, where a large number had gathered and were praying" (Acts 12:12). Prayer meetings are also described in Acts 16 and Acts 20.

Small prayer groups are one important way of restoring prayer to our lives. This chapter focuses on another way, "prayer visits."

When was the last time you invited a family over to your house to pray? It seems strange to me that although Christ is supposed to be the center of our lives—the bond that holds the church together—yet we are uncomfortable with including Him in our social events. We invite people over informally to eat supper, to talk, to play volleyball, or to go swimming; no one is embarrassed to ask someone over for dessert. Yet asking people over to discuss a Christian book, to read a few chapters of the Bible together, or to pray is considered (unless it is part of a regular prayer meeting) virtually a social *faux pas*.

Why? Unlike the old occupations of farming and trades, most modern jobs have set time limits. Television shows exactly fill up half-hour or one-hour time slots. To a great extent, we've tried to compartmentalize Christ the way we do our TV watching. We give Him a two-hour time slot on Sunday mornings, a one-hour time slot for Sunday evening or a week-night prayer group, and perhaps fifteen or twenty minutes a day of private devotions; in all else, Jesus had better not intrude on "our time." But if we take Christ's lordship seriously, we will let Him be a part of our social life as well. I offer four suggestions to make you more comfortable with inviting friends to your home for prayer.

1. If you are inviting one person or a family for prayer and no other activity, it is best to have a specific subject about which to pray. Audrey and I had planned to have only one child, but when Rocky was just a year old, we feared she was pregnant again. She had all the signs, but it could not yet be confirmed. The suspense was unbearable. Finally we invited a couple to pray with us for peace in accepting God's will whatever it might be. The four of us shared a marvelous time. As it turned out, the other couple was somewhat distressed at the same time because they had been wanting to have a child and were unable. We all comforted one another. Afterward Audrey and I enjoyed our first good night's sleep in several days.

Specific prayers can be offered about pending decisions—such as whether to move—and about happy events. Families can be invited over to celebrate an engagement, a graduation, a job offer, or a new car with prayer. The purchase of a house is a great event to celebrate with prayer—especially in a time of "tight" money and high mortgage rates. Having a specific topic of prayer serves two functions: It causes everyone to "get down to business"; otherwise there may be a tendency to chat for some time and prayer is reduced to a quick visit with God rather than a relaxed conversation. Second, everyone will probably feel more comfortable on such an occasion—especially the first few times—if there is a specific reason for coming together for prayer. It may be difficult to say, "Will you come pray with us tomorrow night?" but it's fairly easy to say, "Sandra got a promotion this week, and we're really excited about it. Will you come over and thank God with us tomorrow night?"

2. A second approach is to suggest prayer during an evening visit together. For instance, if you have invited a person or a family for dinner, you can omit the mealtime prayer and tell the company you would prefer to pray after the meal when there is more time. Or, if you have spent the afternoon visiting, say, "I've had such a good time talking

with you today. Would it be all right for us to thank God together?"

Courtesy is important, however. As firmly as I believe in families praying together, there are times it should not be done. If the couple or family is obviously anxious to leave, you are not being charitable by asking them to stay several more minutes to pray, and charity is a higher priority than prayer. Some families are not favorably impressed if they announce, "Well, it's time for us to go," and you respond with, "Hey, I think we all ought to pray for a while." By putting it off, you have implied that you are uncomfortable with prayer, that it is at the bottom of the evening's list of activities, and that the other family's time is not important to you. A suggestion for prayer ideally should come in early or mid-evening; on the other hand, if the family does not seem in a hurry, suggest prayer and gauge their reaction. Closing prayer can be a climax to a special time together.

Another situation in which you will need good judgment is in asking families with small children to pray. If the mother has a crying baby and the father an active toddler, chances are your prayer time together will not draw them much closer to God. Often, however, these are the very people who need an opportunity to pray with others. Therefore, if you volunteer to entertain the children in another room while your spouse prays with the couple, you may be doing a great service for them and for God.

3. A third approach to sharing a prayer time with guests is to have a "prayer and activity" party.

"I want to put together the house."

"Is this all the edge?"

"Libby, help me find a piece of sky with three tabs and one tab holder."

"Marv, are you sure all the pieces are here? I can't find the back half of the red Volkswagen."

Audrey and I once asked several friends to join us for a "prayer and puzzle" party. We worked on jigsaw puzzles until ten o'clock and stopped for devotions and prayer; then those who could stay finished the puzzles afterward.

If jigsaw puzzles are not your forte, how about a "prayer and (homemade) pizza," a "prayer and volleyball," or a "prayer and word games" party?

A person might have two objections to this idea. First, one may ask, "Why does something have to be added to prayer for people to come? Do they really need to be 'bribed'?"

Yes, sometimes they do. I think of it not as a bribe, however, but as a way of putting people at ease. There are still many people who have never attended a small prayer group or engaged in conversational prayer. The word "prayer" to such people connotes stiff, pious phrases to be reserved for church buildings. They know they don't like *that,* and if you invite them to a "prayer meeting," they will reject the idea out-of-hand. If, however, you invite these people to a "prayer and volleyball" party, they know that they do enjoy volleyball. Perhaps, they will reason, a moderate amount of prayer can be endured for an evening of volleyball. When they sit in the prayer group that night, they may become aware of a new way of prayer, a way that is meaningful to them.

After a new Christian attended our prayer group for the first time, she told a friend, "It wasn't the way I thought it would be; in fact, I actually enjoyed it. Once or twice I even thought about talking to God myself!"

The second potential objection to a "prayer and activity" party is that it makes prayer seem relatively less important. If jigsaw puzzles are perceived as the main event of the evening, doesn't that demean prayer?

That is a well-motivated argument. There is no merit in putting on a "sideshow" in order to give people a dose of prayer. *The Wittenburg Door* regularly offers a "Truth Is Stranger Than Fiction" section, and I am as appalled as anyone at churches that advertise "hymn-singing Siamese twins" and "legless gospel pianists" to attract crowds (Those are actual examples). I am pleased when someone is drawn to prayer who otherwise might not have been, but my primary motivation is to include God in my social life as well as my religious life. After all, Jesus performed His first miracle at a wedding feast.

4. A final suggestion for inviting guests over to pray is a "praise evening." I come from a rural "Bible Belt" background where one of God's chief functions—so it seemed—was to provide rain. Every few years that portion of Missouri can be counted on to dry up during July and August; when that occurs, some of the local churches set up prayer meetings to beseech God for rain.

I can't quarrel with this. Some equivalent sort of thing might be good for all of us. An irregular, inconsistent source of income would increase our economic dependence on God, and there's something to be said for that. But one night after our (urban) prayer group had met, I mentioned the curious phenomenon that there had never been, to my knowledge, a prayer meeting about the weather in a good year. In summers when the rains continued to flow, God was taken for granted.

"They ought to have a special praise evening during the years God blesses them," Gwen observed.

"Hey, why don't we do that?" Art suggested.

The idea skyrocketed, and a few weeks later our prayer group sponsored a special praise evening. We spent a half-hour singing hymns of praise interspersed with specific items of thanksgiving for what God had done in the previous year. Several people shared verses of Scripture that speak of God's love, and the thirty of us then prayed conversationally for a half-hour, celebrating God's love. Afterward we served punch for people who wanted to stay and talk. The affair was such a popular success that we held another one several months later.

An effective time for a praise evening is when you or some friends are moving. Just before Audrey and I moved from Missouri to Indiana, we invited about fifteen people to our home for an evening of praise. We sang some songs together, Audrey sang a couple of solos, and I expressed our feelings on the occasion; then we all prayed together for a half-hour. I closed the prayer time by thanking God for a specific act or attribute we appreciated in each person there. It was a moving time for all of us.

Except in unusual circumstances, God does not call us to give up pizza, volleyball, or socializing. But He does want to be the Lord of these activities. If we can let Him be God not only in the religious sphere but in the social and recreational spheres of life as well, we will come closer to "praying without ceasing." As Paul expressed this in his letter to the Colossians: "And whatever you do by word or deed, do it all in the name of the Lord Jesus, through whom you are offering thanks to God the Father" (3:17).

Putting Prayer Into Practice

I have suggested four possibilities for inviting friends to your home to pray: Prayer for a specific event or decision, prayer during a visit, a "prayer and activity" party, or a praise evening. The first two you can sponsor alone; for the latter two, you may very well want the help of a family or two. Above all, do not enter into the "Martha complex" because of one of these activities. Always remember that you are doing this to please God; if housecleaning or food preparation strains your relationship with Christ and family, you are spiritually stalemating. Ask God's forgiveness, ask Him for a change in attitude, and then, if necessary, ask someone to help you.

Prayer in the Closet

15

THE REMAINING CHAPTERS OF THIS BOOK CONCERN THREE VAR-
ieties of prayer: Personal, small-group, and family. Although
prayer is always offered to God, circumstances can alter the
subject matter of it. Aunt Millie's pending visit is an appropriate topic for private prayer, but it would not be a meaningful subject for an entire congregation to hear you pray about,
especially at length.

Whenever I lead a discussion on personal prayer, certain
questions invariably arise, and these two are usually first:
"Does it make any difference how long I pray? Isn't the
quality of my time with God more important than the quantity of time spent with Him?"

It does matter how long you pray. I see the secretaries at
my school daily, yet we don't really know one another from
our customary two minutes of chatter.

All of us are aware how easy it is to speak often with
someone for several months yet never really understand his
or her thoughts and feelings. A single two-or-three-hour
conversation, however, allows time for people to become
open and express their feelings. In a similar way, many
people pray to God for five or ten minutes each day without
developing a healthful, deep relationship with Him.

For most people, however, the solution is not to spend an hour or two each day in prayer. We all feel pressures of time. Andrew Marvell expressed it,

> *But at my back I always hear*
> *Time's wingéd chariot hurrying near.*

Besides, most of us have limited attention spans. So, taking these factors into account, I suggest a possible time pattern for your personal prayer life.

1. You should designate a special time each day when you will spend perhaps fifteen minutes alone with God. This can be as flexible as you need to make it; I generally pray twenty minutes on school days and forty on weekends and in the summer. But it does need to have a high priority. If you are busy during the prayer time—such as attending a child's Little League game—don't try to fulfill your regular prayer then; save it for a quiet time later that day.

2. Arrange a special one-hour (or longer) block of time to spend with God once a week. At that time have in mind different kinds of prayers you want to make and subjects you want to cover, to keep your mind from wandering.

3. Pray short prayers of rejoicing and thanksgiving throughout the day (1 Thessalonians 5:16–18), whether matters are going poorly or well. Thank God for something specific: The work you're getting done, the air conditioner cooling the room, the way the boards in the remodeling project are fitting together, the way the engine is running. Remember that in Christ "all things hold together" (Colossians 1:17). Everything around you that is not collapsing is a result of Christ's influence, even the chair you're sitting in—He keeps its atoms together. The fact that He does this throughout all creation (I've never seen a tree disintegrate) is no reason to neglect to thank Him. "All things" also includes mental abilities and social relationships, such as your marriage.

"Does it make any difference where I pray?" Only to a

certain extent. As a spirit, God can be worshiped anywhere. The short prayers of praise I mentioned above can be delivered anywhere. I have prayed from a hay wagon, a pitcher's mound, a closet, a Massey-Ferguson tractor, a swimming pool, and a ladder, among other places.

Still, for your regular prayer times a set environment is helpful. A standard place helps to fix your mind on the purpose at hand. When Audrey, Rocky, and I enter a neighborhood ice cream store, we immediately approach the cashier and order our cones. We don't stand around inside the door wondering if there's something else we should be doing or what would be the best way to start. Similarly, when you sit at your desk at your chosen time of four o'clock, you know that you're there to pray and not to rest, play with paper clips, or doodle.

That brings up a related question: "Do I need set topics about which to pray?" For regular prayers, you do. Of course, any time a decision or event is weighing heavily on your mind, you should immediately unburden yourself to God; but generally your prayers will be more specific if you have certain topics planned for five of the regular prayer days. From the variety I suggest, choose those that will be most meaningful to you. You can pray for forgiveness of sins, praise and adoration, meditation on Scripture, spiritual help and guidance for yourself, spiritual help and guidance for someone else, physical needs, thankfulness, meditation on hymns or Christian books, requests for wisdom and self-improvement, the events of the day past or the day ahead, family members, the church, or the prayer group.

There is value, I think, in spontaneous prayer; so perhaps you would like to leave two of the days entirely unplanned. I offer my current personal prayer schedule as an example:

SUNDAY: Adoration, preparation for worship

MONDAY: Discursive meditation

TUESDAY: Forgiveness for sins and anticipatory prayer regarding temptation

WEDNESDAY: Spontaneous prayer

THURSDAY: Extended prayer for a specific person, a different one each week

FRIDAY: Writing a letter to God

SATURDAY: The one-hour "special time"

"Should I pray aloud?" For most people, the sound of their own voices gives them heightened awareness that God is a Person who actually hears them. He hears even if we don't pray audibly, but our sensitivity that He is hearing us often improves concentration.

This question is related to the broader subject of our physical attitudes in prayer. C. S. Lewis observes in *The Screwtape Letters* (Letter IV) that most of us are not aware how the position of our bodies affects what we do. The most important physical factor for improving your prayer life is this: Do not let your main prayer time occur *in bed* immediately after awaking or before sleeping. These are good times to pray spontaneously; I often use the night-time in particular to reflect on the day and praise God for what has happened. But beds have a powerful soporific influence.

Moreover, what does this say about your relationship to God? "Father, I'm pretty busy all day, but at night—when I can't do anything important—I'll talk with You." Try telling your spouse that and see the reaction it brings. So try walking outside (especially for praise prayers), sitting, or kneeling while you pray. If you lie down while praying, choose a time of day when you are alert. For all these questions of time, place, and position, the issue is the same: Is the way I pray intended to honor God or to convenience myself?

"Should I pray even when it's difficult?" It is easy to offer a glib "yes" answer, saying that we "owe" this duty to God; or a glib "no" answer, arguing that prayer should not produce guilt. This is a complex question of spiritual motivation.

There are times when circumstances make it difficult to hold to our regular prayer time. When Audrey and I travel to Missouri for a vacation, the eight-hour trip and the excited conversations make it hard to have a regular personal prayer time. We compensate by praying together in the car. Doctors on call and members of the armed services occasionally have days in which finding time to be alert and alone with God is impractical. God is omniscient; He does not judge our desire to please Him solely by the number of times we pray.

On the other hand, prayer is too important in our relationship with the Father to omit lightly. What people usually mean by the question "What if it's difficult to pray?" is not "What if I'm overwhelmed by circumstances?" but rather "What if I don't feel like praying?"

God is our Father, but He is also our Master. As His children, we receive God's blessings; as servants, we are expected to place obedience to Him above personal comfort. If we decide not to pray simply because we don't want to, it would seem we are not being servants to our Master.

Consider whether there is a particular reason for your reluctance to pray. Perhaps a sin has been subconsciously bothering you, such as a lie or a family argument. Promptly tell God you're sorry, and then immediately do what you can to correct the situation (Matthew 5:24). Or perhaps you need a change of routine; try kneeling while praying, or praying outside under a tree in the backyard, or praying in some other different way.

If, however, you simply have an overall reluctance to pray under any condition, you should know the most likely reason why: Satan does not want you to pray. This may sound very cloak-and-daggerish, but it remains true. Often I have heard people remark at the close of a prayer session, "That was so refreshing! I wonder why we don't do it more often?" We don't because Satan is masterful at drawing our attention downward toward thoughts about food, TV, and household chores. Satan can easily find some vague reason for us to avoid prayer. There is only one way to defeat this tactic—by following Colossians 3:2: "Apply your mind to things above, not to things on earth."

When you decide to persist in prayer even on those days when it seems futile, God may bless you in a special way. In *A Second Touch* Keith Miller describes a time when he was expected to speak at a religious conference but felt spiritually drained. Despite misgivings, he decided he had to fulfill his obligation. After giving the address, Keith felt depressed at doing so poorly; but surprisingly, that speech's spiritual effect was as great as for any he had ever given! Several people came and told him how directly his talk had spoken to their lives; he concluded that we do not need to be spiritual giants to worship or represent God.[1]

"Sometimes I don't feel very spiritual when I am finished praying. What's the matter?" Nothing at all. Think of your conversations with a good friend. Sometimes one of you will have some exciting news and the conversation will be invigorating. At other times you have an opportunity to unburden yourself and you feel relieved. But many times, after talking with a close friend, you will "feel" nothing at all. God is a Person, and it is unrealistic to expect our conversations with Him always to be exciting or heartrending any more than our other conversations.

When I first began talking with God at the age of fifteen, I never prayed for anyone else or for forgiveness of sins or for spiritual attributes. All I did, night after night for more than a year, was talk over the day with God. I would tell Him what happened in my first-period class and how I felt about it, then continue through the day. Although now I pray at a considerably deeper level, I have never offered "better" prayers than I did that first year—"better" in the sense of being more earnest and heartfelt. For me to continue to pray that way all the time, however, would be childish, as if I still used baby-talk with Mom and Dad.

You may feel very comfortable with your personal prayer at this point, and that is commendable. But if you do not find

[1](Waco, Tex.: Word Books, 1967).

yourself gradually increasing in spiritual sensitivity and maturity, you need to ignore your comfortable feelings. Christ compares believers to healthy plants; until He's ready to harvest us, we need to grow.

Putting Prayer Into Practice

It's time to make some decisions if you haven't already made them: (1) How many minutes each day do you want to spend with God in a regular prayer time? (2) When is the best time to do this? (3) Where should you do it? (4) On what day each week will you spend a special, longer time with God? (5) What topic will you pray about each day? Put this list by your "prayer spot."

Prayer in the Divided Home   16

THERE ARE TWO TYPES OF HOMES WITH CHRISTIANS: HOMES where everyone of age is a Christian, and homes where at least one member is not. In this chapter I consider households in which at least one member is not a Christian.[1]

It seems that dedicated Christians sometimes misapply Jesus' words in Matthew 10:36: "And a man's enemies will be those who belong to his own household." Some people apparently feel that Christ is *calling* them to a life of enmity with their families. They fall into the kinds of mistakes illustrated in the following dialogue:

"Mom, I'm going to be late for basketball practice! Can't you please drive me to school now?"

"Laurie, that's the second time you've interrupted me. Now I just read a book that says I need to pray at least fifteen minutes a day to keep up my relationship with God, and that's what I'm going to do, whether you like it or not!"

If Laurie's mother will then righteously intone, "Whoever comes to me without hating her children cannot be My disciple," the damage will be nearly complete. In Matthew 10:36

---

[1] In this chapter and the next, the terms "home" and "family" include dormitory and apartment living situations.

Christ is stating a fact rather than giving a command. It is indeed true that many family members are uncomfortable around one who is a committed Christian; Christ Himself was rejected by His brothers until after His resurrection. But we are commanded in Romans 12:18, "if possible, so far as it depends on you, live at peace with everyone."

The opposite approach, however, is a great deal more common. Christians often feel that to keep from offending their non-Christian roommates or relatives, they should refrain from displaying their relationship with God.

When the New Testament admonishes that praying to impress other Christians is detestable, that certainly does not preclude all prayer in the presence of Christians. Similarly, while we should not pray before non-Christians in order to appear more religious than they, we should not needlessly avoid *all* prayer around them. Some New Testament examples encourage prayer before unbelievers. Christ specifically stated that His prayer before Lazarus' tomb was intended for unbelievers' hearing: "Father, I thank Thee for having heard Me, and I know that Thou dost always hear Me; but on account of the people around here I said this, so that they may believe that Thou hast sent Me" (John 11:41–42).

Our prayers do not need to be blatantly evangelistic, of course. Consider the example of Paul and Silas in prison at Philippi: "About midnight Paul and Silas were praying and singing hymns to God, and the prisoners were listening to them" (Acts 16:25).

The second part of that verse is important. Paul and Silas were aware of the attention they were receiving from the other prisoners—how else could Luke know they were listening? But Paul and Silas did not decide in the presence of non-Christians to forgo hymn-singing and oral prayer.

These biblical examples have implications for Christians in a non-Christian environment. First, you might wish at some point to explain to non-Christians in your home that your prayer time is a conversation with Someone you love and enjoy. And, therefore, while you like to have uninterrupted time in this Person's company, you are willing for it to be halted for something important in the same way any other conversation would be.

Once my college roommate and I were praying together when the telephone rang in the middle of his sentence. I wondered what he'd do: Rapidly end our prayer time? Wait till the phone stopped? Try to pray through it? To my surprise, he said, "Just a minute, Lord," and went to the phone. He answered it, talked a few moments, came back to his bed, and unpretentiously resumed his conversation with God.

God is holy; He should be regarded with awe and reverence. Yet God Himself, in the person of Christ, taught that religious activities should not stop one from doing good works. Christ deliberately healed a man on the Sabbath. And Clarence Jordan, the brilliant "Cotton Patch" translator, speculates in *Cotton Patch Parables of Liberation* that perhaps one of Christ's themes in the Good Samaritan parable was the primacy of good works over religious activities. The priest and Levite might have been on their way to perform temple duties—an honorable objective—but ignoring the wounded man would still have been wrong. Similarly, if a child falls down and cuts his knee but can't get a Band-Aid or a hug because "Mommy's praying and can't be interrupted," we are elevating prayer to a level God does not intend.

So families and roommates should be made aware that we can be both prayerful and available. In addition, we should not hesitate to pray in front of them if circumstances call for it. I think a particularly appropriate time is when we have done something wrong and are apologizing to the roommate or family member for it. The other person should realize that we are as upset about disappointing God as about angering him or her. We might handle the situation this way:

"Cheryl, I'm sorry about getting mad at you this afternoon."

"Well, Ann, I was pretty mad, too."

"Cheryl, I really feel I've let down two people—you and God. I'm going to ask Him to forgive me now, and since you're involved I'd like to ask you to listen."

"Okay."

"God, I'm sorry about letting you and Cheryl down today. I acted as though I'm perfect, as though I hadn't ever been late to do something. Father, thank You for forgiving my proud attitude. Amen."

Another time to pray around non-Christian roommates and relatives is when a Christian friend comes to visit. If the two of you decide to pray together and the subject is not a private matter, you do not need to ask a non-Christian in the room to leave. If he is reading a magazine or eating a sandwich and prefers to stay in the same room, that's fine.

I've had to generalize a great deal in this chapter; I am aware that in many situations my suggestions will not work. For instance, a former student of mine became a Christian in a home where her father forbade prayer or Bible study. What does one do then? My advice for an instance like that sums up the guidelines for all divided-home situations: Remember above everything else that Christ is your Lord. Beyond that—well, God is flexible enough to bless different responses. In Babylon, three young Israelites were expected to bow down to an idol; they refused, and God protected them from the fiery furnace (Daniel 3). Naaman, a Syrian army captain, was expected to bow down to an idol. Yet Naaman asked Elisha, the prophet of God, for permission to bow down, and permission was granted (2 Kings 5:18).

You may draw your own conclusions, but in deciding to what extent your Christianity should be displayed before an unbelieving family, you need not rely solely on your intuition. "If any one of you lacks wisdom, let him ask God, who gives to everyone without reserve and without reproach" (James 1:5).

Putting Prayer Into Practice

I don't advise telling your roommate or spouse in a general way "I'll pray for you" when he is going to take a test or look for a job. He can't understand what good that will do. A better way is to demonstrate how you keep up a relationship with God under all circumstances. If God has prompted you to do something special or improve in a certain aspect and the spouse or roommate notices, you can tell him that's something you've been praying about and—if he's agreeable— you can thank God in front of him for changing you.

Prayer in the Christian Home

17

THERE ARE HARDLY ANY CHRISTIAN HOMES IN THE UNITED States. By "Christian home," I mean a household in which the basic orientation is Christian, a home where the members regularly edify, instruct, pray for, pray with, and praise God with one another. Many people assume that a home is a Christian place if all its members are Christian; one might as well assume that a church building is a barn if all its members are farmers. A building's function is determined not by the backgrounds of those in it, but by their relationships there.

Like many other people in the evangelical community, I grew up in a home where the members were religious but did not regularly edify one another. We had regular mealtime prayers, church prayers, and a "Christmas prayer" each year, but otherwise we never prayed together, never allowed anyone else to hear us praying, or even indicated that we did pray.

I still remember how shocked I was the first time I heard someone in my family pray. When I was eight years old, my seventeen-year-old sister was driving me to school, and the car was sliding in the snow. She was afraid the car would slide into a ditch and quickly prayed, "God, please help us!" My vivid memories of that event indicate the effect prayer can have on children.

For you who live in families where all the members of believing age are Christians, what is your responsibility toward one another? A passage in the Old Testament speaks directly to this question.

"Hear, O Israel, the LORD our God is one LORD, and you shall love the LORD your God with all your heart, with all your soul, and with all your strength. These words with which I am now charging you shall be written on your heart; and you shall impress them deeply upon your children; you shall talk of them when you are sitting at home, while you walk on the road, when you lie down, and when you get up" (Deuteronomy 6:4-7).

Since we live in the Christian era, we should substitute Christ for the words of the law. Therefore the charge to us is that Christ "shall be written on your heart; and you shall impress [Him] deeply upon your children." I could expound at length how to do this: By studying the Gospels intensely with your children to reveal Christ's lifestyle and person to them, instilling Christ's attitudes, showing them how to help the sick and the poor. But that is beyond the scope of this book, so I will give attention only to the implications for prayer.

First, our children need to know to whom they are praying. From our teaching they will know the Jesus of the Gospels and picture Him in heaven; they will also easily understand that He has a Father there. Audrey and I have tried to explain the unity of God and Christ by telling Rocky that though they are separate personalities, they can enter one another's bodies and minds to become one Person. A young child also needs to know God's attributes, especially His omnipresence, His creative power, and His love. The child should be told that Jesus showed us what He was like in the Bible, and He wants us to share what we're thinking and feeling with Him.

We can teach children these concepts directly; how to communicate sincerely and humbly with God, we can't. We will have to show them. By all means, children should hear the parents pray, both separately and together. If the parents seem to enjoy prayer and pray often, the child will come to regard it as important. Far too often parents confine their prayer time with children to bedtime prayers, which often become a ritual "signal for bedtime" of the kind we noted in an earlier chapter. If children never hear their parents pray at any other time or place, they eventually assume that prayer is something only for bedtime that they will outgrow.

I recommend against "set prayers"—"Now I lay me down to sleep . . ."—for the same reason. The child never hears *us* pray that way.

What sort of prayers should our children hear from us? Happiness at what God has done, first of all. We should praise God in front of our children for creating heaven and imagine what it might be like. (After several discussions with me over the freedom from injury and illness in heaven, Rocky asked, "Do you know why nobody ever bumps his nose in heaven?" When I answered no, he said, "Because it doesn't have any walls!")

Moreover, God can be praised for His works recorded in the Bible, including Jesus' miracles and His atoning death. Children can understand forgiveness of sin at a surprisingly early age. When Rocky was barely four, he saw Audrey "white out" a word at the typewriter. Praying with me later that day, Rocky said, "Daddy, sin is like a word on signs all over the world, and when Jesus died, it whited out the words on all those signs." I could have explained justification for a decade and not come up with a simile as good as that!

Children should regularly hear us express thankfulness. They should hear us thank God for them, for our spouses, for good events and bad. I mentioned Rocky's "Thank you that we don't have enough money to buy a house" in the preface. He had simply heard thankfulness so much that he felt any occasion, no matter what, was a time to thank God.

Another type of prayer very important for children to hear is a parent's asking God for forgiveness for a specific sin. Many books today recommend that parents apologize to children whom they've wrongfully punished or belittled; the idea has merit, particularly in our efforts toward humility. But I think it is at least equally important for parents to apologize to God in front of children. The sin does not have to be child-directed, merely something children saw us do.

There is a four-way intersection near our home that inexplicably has "No Turn on Red" signs at each corner. I think the signs are senseless, so once when the two cars in front of ours turned right on the red light, I did too. Audrey gently reproved me, but I pointed out to her that Christians do not need to obey stupid laws, only intelligent ones. (That "gift of rationalization" again!) Before I drove another mile, however, I realized my sinfulness and admitted it to my family. I should then have prayed to God before them to emphasize bowing down to God's Spirit; I didn't, but I sin often enough that I'm sure there will soon be another opportunity to pray in front of them. When children repeatedly see their parents submitting to God's authority, they will more likely also submit to His authority and to their parents' as well.

The matter of apologizing to God applies to relationships between spouses and roommates also. That prayer relationship is difficult to maintain, however, especially with a spouse. I suppose in marriage we tend to see our husbands and wives only in that way—as husbands and wives—rather than as Christian brothers and sisters.

The first major spiritual hurdle Audrey and I had to overcome in our marriage occurred during our third year together. It was a time of intense spiritual growth for me, and almost every week at prayer group I had some new understanding of Christ to share with the Christians there. After several weeks of this, Audrey sobbed to me one night, "How come you never tell me anything that God's done for you? You always wait till the group's together, and it makes me feel like I'm not your spiritual partner." She was right. Now we consistently try to edify each other.

What I've been saying comes together in this: Most of us

generally relate to fellow Christians only in the primary asso-
ciation we have with them. My wife's boss is a professor at
the local university; he is also an elder in our church. It is
difficult for Audrey to relate to him as a Christian brother,
because the employer-employee relationship overshadows
any other relationship. To have effective prayer in the home,
you will have to look at your spouse, roommate, or children
in a new light: They are members of the body of Christ with
you.

Putting Prayer Into Practice

1. One way Audrey and I have strengthened our Christian
relationship is by taking Communion at home together, a
practice suggested by Pat Boone in his book *The Honeymoon
Is Over.* [1]

Audrey and I prepare the grape juice and cracker, then
spend several minutes praying together. We gain a real sense
of closeness; in addition, it gives us more opportunities to
contemplate the sacrificial love of Christ than our own
church provides. Like C. S. Lewis, I find that a monthly
observance of Communion is not frequent enough for me to
praise God properly for His redemption.

(If you belong to a denomination in which the celebration
of the Lord's Supper or the Eucharist is normally adminis-
tered only by ordained clergy, you will have to decide
whether denominational tradition outweighs the spiritual
benefits.)

2. When there are children in the home, husbands and
wives need to take an especially active interest in each other's
time alone with Christ. A thoughtful spouse might say, "I'm
going to take the kids out for a walk. This would be a good
time for you to pray, wouldn't it?" Busy mothers particularly appreciate these special occasions alone with God.

[1](Nashville: Thomas Nelson, 1980).

Prayer in the Group

18

IN SOME CIRCUMSTANCES SMALL-GROUP PRAYER CAN BE AS important as personal prayer. Audrey and I met weekly for more than five years with a group of eight to ten committed Christians for one-and-a-half hours of prayer, Bible study, Communion, and hymn-singing. It was this group, more than any other factor, that God used for our spiritual growth.

When we first began meeting, however, the group was primarily concerned, not with prayer, but with Bible study. Our prayers were a series of short requests sandwiched between hymn-singing and studying Scripture. As time went on, different members of the group became intrigued by the concepts of servanthood and pleasing God.

I became especially interested in worship. I was perplexed by the fact that the heavenly saints in Revelation are pictured as constantly praising and adoring God; yet none of us on earth knew how to do that. All we could do was ask God for good health and good gas mileage! Our situation was described in the sixth verse of the hymn "O Worship the King."

The humbler creation, though feeble their lays,
With true adoration shall lisp to thy praise.

Except that we couldn't even lisp; we were mute.

Eventually prayer came to be the focus of our time together, although other elements of worship were retained. I am heartily in favor of Bible studies, fellowship meals, and choir meetings, but I think prayer groups are far more important for three reasons. First, God commands prayer more often and more strongly than any other specific element of worship. Second, prayer is vastly underrated by the church today in a way most other elements of worship are not. Third, it is mainly through prayer—especially small-group prayer—that a church will begin to transform itself from an organization into an organism. A church member can easily hide his thoughts and feelings during a Bible study by focusing on objective facts. ("In what year did you say the Book of Leviticus was written?") As people grow comfortable with talking to God in the presence of each other, however, they display their real joys and concerns.

There are some guidelines to follow in establishing and maintaining an effective prayer group. The most important is to become involved with a group of Christians who are seriously dedicated to Christ. There are few things more spiritually frustrating than meeting with a group that would rather visit and play with the children than pray.

Beyond that requirement, seven factors can help your group avoid potential pitfalls.

1. Start on time. If the prayer group meets from 7:30 to 8:30, and some of the members don't arrive until 7:45, one-fourth of the time available for prayer has been wasted. Moreover, if other members were on time and have been waiting fifteen minutes for someone else, they are not likely to be in a worshipful mood. If a person or couple are perpetually late, talk with them privately about it.

2. Develop a worshipful attitude at the beginning. Psalm 100:4 commands the people of Israel to *"enter into his gates with thanksgiving and into his courts with praise."* Sometimes we don't enter worship services with praise; many of us

are still filled with the day's concerns and need a few minutes to collect our thoughts. A hymn or short devotional reading at the beginning of your time together can effectively turn people's thoughts toward God. Besides various New Testament passages, I have used selections from *Prayer: Conversing with God* (Rosalind Rinker), *Sidewalk Prayers* (Orlando Tibbetts), *Crowded Pews and Lonely People* (M. L. Jacobsen), *The Best of A. W. Tozer,* and assorted thoughts from *Christian Digest* and C. S. Lewis's works. The selection should be short—not more than two pages—and Christ-centered.

3. The group should have a leader every time it comes together. This may or may not be the same person each time; there is value in having different people lead, because preparing a short devotional meditation is a good opportunity to gain wisdom. Our prayer group in Missouri rotated homes as meeting places for a time, and a person from the "host home" prepared the meditation. In our current prayer group, I read through a book of devotion during my own time and mark sections that members might find stimulating. Each week I give the book to a different member to prepare a meditation for the following week.

4. You should include all types of prayer in your sessions. This does not mean each session will include every category —praise for works of God, thanksgiving for blessings and trials, petition for physical needs, petition for spiritual needs, sorrow for sin, and adoration of God. But over a period of several weeks these and other kinds of prayer should appear. A group can pray about problems so incessantly that it loses sight of God. This is particularly a danger when all the group's members are from the same congregation; in my experience, interdenominational prayer groups are usually more spiritually stimulating than intracongregational ones. ones.

5. People should be encouraged to share their relevant experiences of the preceding week. This could be a decision they are facing or one in which they felt God was guiding; a

meaningful Scripture; a new understanding of God; a selection from a Christian book; or an answered prayer. This is entirely in accord with the New Testament pattern of worship as exhibited in 1 Corinthians 14:26: "When you meet together, each one contributes his part." But the leader must keep a firm hand on the reins, making sure gregarious members do not waste time with pointless jokes and stories.

6. Members should keep in mind that there are two purposes of group prayer: Worshiping God and edifying one another. Therefore some prayers that might be important "in the closet" should be left there. A woman in one of our groups used to pray long prayers for her elderly grandfather's health and welfare. Since the other members did not know the grandfather and were unlikely ever to meet him, they found it difficult to agree with her in prayer. That does not entirely preclude prayer for such a situation; if the woman were driving across the state the next week to visit her grandfather, her prayer requests would have meaning for the group members. They could pray for her in giving words of encouragement and could, if the situation warranted it, send money or food.

7. The cohesion of the group will be stronger if the members do other activities together in addition to praying. Occasionally sharing Communion elevates Christ; sharing *"agape meals"* encourages smoother interpersonal relationships. Our current prayer group visited a nursing home to sing hymns; this helped us to avoid self-centeredness.

Maintaining a vital prayer group, like a vital marriage, takes work and commitment. But it's unquestionably worth it. Thanks to what I've learned from God and other people in small-group prayer, I am no longer mute in my admiration for God; I can lisp His praise.

Putting Prayer Into Practice

1. Perhaps you would like to start a prayer group in your home, but don't know how to bring people together. First,

there are probably a few people in your congregation who would be interested. Ask around until you find them. The four or five of you can begin meeting together and ask God to guide you to others in the community who are interested in worshipful prayer. One way to discover them is to look for committed Christians at your various jobs; tell them what your prayer group does before inviting them. Another way to find interested Christians is to call the pastors of two or three other churches in the area. State the purpose of your group and the time and place you meet, and ask them if they would be willing to put a notice about your group in the church bulletin or weekly newsletter (including a phone number for information). Remember that ministers are "fishers of men" and may fear that you want to steal fish from their tank; if they seem hesitant, assure them your desire is only to pray with fellow believers. Usually eight to fifteen people is the best size for a prayer group.

2. One place where a group is already gathered is an adult Sunday school class. If you attend one, perhaps you could discuss with the teacher the possibility of having conversational prayer during the closing ten minutes each week. Or possibly the class could engage in a study of prayer, spending half the class period each week actually praying together.

Beyond Gethsemane 19

But be doers of the word, and not deluders of yourselves by merely listening; for whoever hears the message without acting upon it is similar to the man who observes his own face in a mirror; he takes a look at himself and goes off and promptly forgets how he looks (James 1:22–24).

MY ULTIMATE PURPOSE IN WRITING THIS BOOK IS TO CHALLENGE you to evaluate your relationship with God. It is easier to read about prayer than to pray—much easier. I have prayed that this book will be useful to you, that you will ever more strongly attempt to please God in your prayers. Christ's moving prayer in Gethsemane was an act of preparation; if He had not gone beyond it to the cross, His prayer would have been for nothing. Similarly, your time in reading this book has been preparation for the task of pleasing God.

So where do you go now? What lies beyond Gethsemane? I have purposely divided most of these chapters into two sections, the text and the practical suggestions. I recommend that occasionally (perhaps once every couple of months) you thumb through the "Putting Prayer Into Practice" sections. Ask God to give you wisdom (James 1:5) in deciding what you need. Do not try to put all your newly learned methods into practice at once. As I have stated, varieties of prayers are not nearly as important as simply expressing your love and gratitude to God.

It is important, however, to try to develop your prayer life in all the aspects I have emphasized in the last four chapters: Private, home, and group prayer. Circumstances vary, of course; you cannot really develop an effective home prayer life if you are the only Christian in your household, or an effective group prayer life if you have invited a dozen friends and none of them is interested. On the other hand, it is very easy—and very selfish—for people experiencing a renewed relationship with God in prayer not to bother to share that with others in their church or family.

I opened this book by showing that God is not a vending machine. Having examined the implications of this statement through seventeen chapters, we then confront the obvious question, "If God is not a vending machine, then what *is* He?" More precisely, *who* is He?

God is the Creator and Father who loves us so much that He wants to make us into new beings—sparkling, scintillating, brilliant.

And we are eager for Him to do that—in heaven. On earth, however, most of us resist God's attempts to make us into new creatures. In 2 Corinthians 5:17, Paul doesn't say what we seem to feel, that in heaven we will become new creatures. Instead, the apostle writes, "If anyone is in Christ, he *is* a new creation." Our metamorphosis is already taking place.

But, like a dog being dusted with flea powder, we fight the improvement. The dog ignores the long-term benefit (flea-lessness), which it can't fully understand, in favor of short-term pleasure (escaping the powder). And we ignore the long-term benefit of prayer (our perfecting) in favor of vending-machine gratification.

We want to use prayer to fulfill our desires; God wants to use prayer to fulfill His desires for us. The first way is easier, more natural; the second is less traveled by. But it will make all the difference.